# MILTON AND MELVILLE

*Paradise Lost*, illustrated by John Martin, 1833. Courtesy of The Free Library of Philadelphia

John Martin, *Satan Exalted Sat*

# MILTON
## and MELVILLE

by
### *HENRY F. POMMER*

COOPER SQUARE PUBLISHERS, INC.
NEW YORK
1970

Originally Published and Copyright 1950 by
University of Pittsburgh Press
Published 1970 by Cooper Square Publishers, Inc.
59 Fourth Avenue, New York, N. Y. 10003
Standard Book No. 8154-0338-0
Library of Congress Catalog Card No. 70-122752

*Printed in U.S.A. by*
NOBLE OFFSET PRINTERS, INC.
NEW YORK 3, N. Y.

# ACKNOWLEDGEMENTS

*"That lasting temper of all true, candid men—a seeker, not a finder yet."*
*—"Hawthorne and His Mosses,"*
*XIII, 138*

AHAB regretted his dependence upon his fellow men. I have found my dependence a source of stimulating and heart-warming associations, and I am glad for this opportunity to express my gratitude.

Numerous librarians have shown helpfulness and courtesy beyond the call of duty. In particular I wish to record my appreciation of the aid received from the staff of the Houghton Library of Harvard University, Mr. Gilbert Troxell of the Yale University Library, Mr. Richard S. Hill of the Library of Congress, Miss Adelaide Smith and Mr. Wilmer R. Leech of the New York Public Library, Miss Virginia Warren, Librarian to the late Frank J. Hogan, and Mrs. Catharine J. Pierce and Mrs. Dorothea D. Reeves of the Swarthmore College Library. For permission to examine association and manuscript material in their possession I am grateful to Mr. Alexander O. Vietor and to Melville's four charming granddaughters, Mrs. Katharine G. Binnian, Mrs. E. B. Chapin, Mrs. Eleanor Melville Metcalf, and Mrs. Frances T. Osborne. Authorities of the Houghton Library and of the New York Public Library have aided with permission to quote manuscript material in their collections.

Notes and bibliography indicate most of my debts to fellow scholars. Two obligations, however, could not be expressed in any note, and appropriately appear here; they are to John Bradshaw for his *Concordance to the Poetical Works of John Milton*, and to Professor Frank Allen Patterson and French Rowe Fogle for their *Index to the Columbia Edition of the Works of John Milton*. An even

v

greater weakness is the inability of footnotes to show the assistance which I have received from Miss Frances Blackburn and Professor Lydia Baer of Swarthmore College, from my mother, Elizabeth Pommer Shields, and from Professor Stanley T. Williams, who directed my writing of the dissertation on which this book is based. That work was presented for the degree of Doctor of Philosophy in Yale University. The present book is a complete rewriting of the dissertation. No page has remained unchanged; much new material has been added; much has been omitted; several chapters have been wholly rewritten. Part of the work of revision was facilitated by the anonymous criticism of a reader at Yale University, by the kindly advice of Professor Walter McKellar, and by comments from Professors R. C. Bald, David Daiches, Charles W. Jones, Henry A. Myers, Stanley S. Swartley, and Harold Thompson. To which of all these persons my debt is greatest I might be in doubt, but I am sure that whereas this study owes many of its facts to the persons already named, it owes its very existence to Bessie Westerman Pommer, the helper whose help has meant the most to me.

## OF MATTERS BIBLIOGRAPHICAL

I have tried to avoid superfluity and ostentation in the notes. I have also tried to reduce the number of distractions caused by superior numerals, and have therefore deferred all consecutive references to a single source until the end of the series. Thus, although a particular fact or quotation may at first glance appear unverifiable through the notes, its source will be found in the next note to the text.

Bibliographical information about each work referred to is given in the first reference, as well as in the concluding Bibliography. All mentions between that Alpha and this Omega are by author's last name and book's short title.

Italics in quotations are mine, if there is no note to the contrary.

Unless otherwise indicated, all references to Melville's works are to *The Works of Herman Melville*, Constable Edition (London, 1922-1924), 16 volumes. References to this text are by the titles of the volumes concerned, except that the title of the work concerned and the volume number are given in the cases of volumes X (*The*

*Piazza Tales*), XIII (*Billy Budd and Other Prose Pieces*), and XVI (*Poems, Containing Battle-Pieces, John Marr and Other Sailors, Timoleon, and Miscellaneous Poems*).

*Paradise Lost, Paradise Regained,* and *Samson Agonistes* are referred to by their initial letters. Unless otherwise noted, all quotations from Milton's poetry are from *The Poetical Works of John Milton,* ed. the Rev. Henry J. Todd; The Second Edition (London, 1809), 7 volumes. This edition was chosen for reasons given in Appendix A. Quotations from Milton's prose are from *The Prose Works of John Milton,* ed. Rufus Wilmot Griswold (Philadelphia, 1845), 2 volumes. This edition was chosen because of its popularity in Melville's day. Numerals following titles of Milton's poems refer to Book (if any) and line; in the case of his prose, they refer to volume and page in Griswold's edition.

The following abbreviations have been used in the notes and Bibliography:

| | |
|---|---|
| *Am. Lit.*—*American Literature* | N.Y.—New York City |
| E.A.D.—Evert Augustus Duyckinck | N.Y.P.L.—New York Public Library |
| H.M.—Herman Melville | U.P.—University Press |

Publishers of magazines and books have allowed the use of quotations from material which they have copyrighted. To the following the author wishes to express appreciation:

American Book Company, New York, for selections from *Herman Melville: Representative Selections* (1938) by Willard Thorp.

Appleton-Century-Crofts, Inc., New York, for a selection from *A Milton Handbook* (1941) by James Holly Hanford.

*The Atlantic Monthly,* Boston, for a selection from "Moby Dick" (June, 1948) by Somerset Maugham.

The Bobbs-Merrill Company, Inc., Indianapolis, for selections from *The Delight of Great Books* (1928) by John Erskine.

Ginn and Company, Boston, for a selection from *Literature and American Life* (1936) by Percy H. Boynton.

Harcourt, Brace and Company, Inc., New York, for a selection from *Herman Melville* (1929) by Lewis Mumford.

The Macmillan Company, New York, for a selection from *Herman Melville* (1926) by John Freeman and a selection from *A Half-Day's Ride* (1932) by Padraic Colum.

*The New England Quarterly,* Brunswick, for a selection from "The Dark Angel: The Tragedy of Herman Melville" (October, 1932) by George C. Homans.

G. P. Putnam's Sons, New York, for a selection from *Are Men Equal?* (1945) by Henry Alonzo Myers.

*The publication of this study
has been facilitated by
a grant from
Allegheny College*

# CONTENTS

*"A modest pursuit after Knowledge."*
—*Addison on* Paradise Lost *in
the* Spectator, *No. CCCXXXIX.*

ix

# ILLUSTRATIONS

*"You involuntarily took an oath with yourself to
find out what that marvellous painting meant."*
—Moby-Dick, *I, 13.*

# MILTON AND MELVILLE

# CHAPTER ONE

# SEEDS IN A FERTILE SOIL

> "*Something I remember having
> seen in print, though the
> book I cannot recall.*"
> —Billy Budd, *XIII, 33.*

> Homage to him
> His debtor band, innumerable as waves
> Running all golden from an eastern sun,
> Joyfully render, in deep reverence
> Subscribe, and as they speak their Milton's name,
> Rays of his glory on their foreheads bear.
> —George Meredith: "Milton"

With these lines Raymond Dexter Havens introduced his study
of the influence of Milton on English poetry,[1] and with them may
well begin this contribution to the study of Milton's influence on
American literature. Or should this work be called a contribution
towards *The Road to Albemarle*—to borrow one of Melville's en-
chanted isles—which a later John Livingston Lowes may some
day write about the American creator of ancient mariners? Certainly Milton's influence on Herman Melville can be regarded as a
part of both wholes; yet other purposes can also be found in this
study, and readers can come to it with more limited desires. Some
readers may hope to find here both a testing and an amplifying of
brief, earlier statements about Melville's debt to Milton. They may
hope to learn merely what channels Milton's works trenched in
Melville's mind, what lines of association were cut there by the
seventeenth-century poet. But probably they may wish also to

1

learn how those lines have affected the sixteen volumes of Melville's collected works, what passages show what kinds of influence, and how the various types of influence help to explain the development of Melville's art. Some readers may even feel that, though they recognize the significance of similarities, they must push on to the significance of differences. Others may hope that this study of some of Melville's mental habits and artistic techniques will include generalizations which will remain valid even if applied to thought and art far beyond the range of Milton's influence on Melville, for "this new world here sought is stranger far than his, who stretched his vans from Palos. It is the world of mind; wherein the wanderer may gaze round, with more of wonder than Balboa's band roving through the golden Aztec glades."[2]

Our gaze must not be circumscribed; each page must be consistent with the realization that

> we are not concerned with examining a "literary influence" in the sense in which that term has been deadened by scholarly misuse. The conventional assumption that you can find what produced a writer by studying earlier writers was refuted, long before the Ph.D. thesis was stillborn, by *The American Scholar*. Emerson knew that each age turns to particular authors of the past, not because of the authors but because of its own needs and preoccupations that those authors help make articulate.[3]

The purposes of the study of literary influence must, of course, vary with the nature of the works examined; the problems and fruits of literary source-hunting likewise differ from author to author. In the study of Shakespeare, for example, scholars have found many influential literary sources of his works, but his personal life and its effects on his writing remain elusive. In the case of Melville, on the other hand, the literary sources are probably fewer and less important, whereas the personal roots of his writing are conspicuous. That Melville transferred a great deal of material to his books from direct reactions to his physical environment is clear from careful examinations of that environment, whether the examinations are made through Melville's journals and letters or through records left by other persons.[4] And it is precisely because so much of Melville's writing is autobiographical, and because so much more seems so, that one is often surprised to learn just how much Melville's books do rely on literary sources.

Yet this reliance is hardly to be wondered at. In the first place, while writing books like *Typee*, *White Jacket*, and *Clarel*, Melville must have discovered that his memory needed assistance in reconstructing his life in the South Seas, on a United States frigate, and in the Holy Lands. He was forced to consult other men's books if he was to give his own the fulness of detail that lends authenticity and the accuracy of detail that lends authority. It must have been an easy step from consulting books for information once learned at first hand, to using the same books for supplementary information. In the second place, Melville's experiences, even when perfectly remembered, were sometimes too dull to make dramatic reading, as in the case of his life aboard the *United States*. They then needed supplementation from what could be borrowed with minor or major adaptations.[5] In the third place, Melville was not merely a writer of description and narration, concerned solely with a need for visual and historical details. He was also a writer of exposition, interested in characters, in ideas, and in a style that could change to serve description, narration, exposition, and their innumerable interminglings. His thinking about persons, about various branches of philosophy, and about literary art was greatly facilitated by his reading. Finally, Melville did not write an *Alice in Wonderland* or *Songs of Innocence* on the one hand, nor a *French Revolution* or *American Notes* on the other. What he wanted to write, and did write, required a different use of sources from that needed by some authors. The extent to which Melville's borrowing for any of his needs was conscious or unconscious is irrelevant at this point. For the moment the important idea is that in order ✳ to write better books than his unaided memory or his unaided thinking would have permitted, Melville was forced to draw on the works of other authors.

But whether Melville was conscious or unconscious of his borrowings is not always irrelevant, nor always past finding out. Certainly Melville was both a reader and a collector of books from an early age; certainly he valued books themselves, acquaintance with them, and their general influence upon his writing. For these statements there are several types of evidence.

Melville's earliest publication, "Fragments from a Writing-Desk," was peppered with unripe fruits of learning—quotations, references, allusions. In his last work, *Billy Budd*, the same fruits are no less significant for their being riper, for their being more often camouflaged from the superficial eye.[6] The intermediate works show the same traits to a greater or less degree. Similarly, from earliest to last work there are characters who are unusually well-read, some of them characters who are generously autobiographical. Redburn and Pierre, for example, tell us more about their author's youth than do any other characters, and both Redburn and Pierre browse long hours in the libraries of book-loving sires. Redburn, Ishmael, Omoo, and White Jacket give the broad outlines of Melville's life at sea; Redburn, Omoo, and White Jacket are ardent readers. These characters have additional readers among their closest friends—Mr. Jones, Dr. Long Ghost, Jack Chase, Nord, and Lemsford. Then there are Taji, guilty of "remote, unguarded allusions to Belles-Lettres affairs";[7] Babbalanja, "much given to quotations from ancient and obsolete authorities";[8] Captain Vere, who never went to sea "without a newly replenished library, compact but of the best";[9] and Derwent, Rolfe, and less prominent readers.

In addition to this evidence from Melville's fiction, never to be taken as literal autobiography, there is other evidence to prove that he was justified in portraying himself as a persistent reader. We know, for example, that he could have met at sea fully as many well-read sailors, and fully as many ships' libraries and scattered volumes as he mentions in his fiction. Then too, we know that Melville spent typical evenings reading with his wife, that he frequently chatted and corresponded about books, and that, during the period of his most significant writing, his most intimate friends were active readers like Evert A. Duyckinck and Nathaniel Hawthorne. We know also that Melville borrowed books from the New York Society Library and from Duyckinck's collection of more than fifteen thousand volumes—a Vatican, as Melville once called it. Finally, there is abundant evidence that Melville bought books during most of his life, amassing by the time of his death a library "which was a large one for the time."[10] Some volumes of that library have been preserved—not, unfortunately, the Milton.[11] Melville's marks in the surviving volumes prove how attentively he read what interested him.

4

All this considerable evidence, which could be given in much fuller detail, demonstrates that Melville recognized the pleasure of reading and its value in making men. He also recognized its value in making books. It is true that in *Pierre* Melville elaborates the truth that a great author is made by what he has thought, not by what he has read:

A varied scope of reading, little suspected by his friends, and randomly acquired by a random but lynx-eyed mind, in the course of the multifarious, incidental bibliographic encounterings of almost any civilised young inquirer after Truth; this poured one considerable contributory stream into that bottomless spring of original thought which the occasion and time had caused to burst out in [Pierre] . . . . He congratulated himself upon all his cursory acquisitions of this sort; ignorant that in reality to a mind bent on producing some thoughtful thing of absolute Truth, all mere reading is apt to prove but an obstacle hard to overcome; and not an accelerator helpingly pushing him along. . . .

He did not see that there is no such thing as a standard for the creative spirit; that no one great book must ever be separately regarded, and permitted to domineer with its own uniqueness upon the creative mind; but that all existing great works must be federated in the fancy; and so regarded as a miscellaneous and Pantheistic whole; and then,—without at all dictating to his own mind, or unduly biasing it any way,—thus combined, they would prove simply an exhilarative and provocative to him. He did not see, that even when thus combined, all was but one small mite, compared to the latent infiniteness and inexhaustibility in himself.[12]

But Melville did not always emphasize originality at the expense of literary influences, as quotations from a period earlier than *Pierre* or *Moby-Dick* will demonstrate. In *Mardi* and *Redburn* Melville had emphasized his own and other authors' debts to the past. This emphasis and the shift to that in *Pierre* can be traced directly to a shift in Melville's method of composition. In *Mardi*, a book of ill-digested eclecticism, Melville had incurred considerable debts himself—for example, by quoting Sir Roger L'Estrange extensively but without credit.[13] In the later *Moby-Dick* and *Pierre*, however, Melville was more original in the sense that he had thoroughly assimilated his literary sources, redyeing and respinning them before weaving them into his own fabrics.[14] The passage just quoted from *Pierre* suggests Melville's awareness of the increased self-reliance underlying his emphasis on originality. Similarly, the following quotations suggest his awareness of his own borrowings underlying his emphasis on indebtedness.

5

In *Mardi*, for example, the hero's exclamation, "Ah! how the old Sagas run through me!" is later amplified:

> In me, many worthies recline, and converse. I list to St. Paul who argues the doubts of Montaigne; Julian the Apostate cross-questions Augustine. . . . My memory is a life beyond birth; my memory, my library of the Vatican, its alcoves all endless perspectives, eve-tinted by cross-lights from Middle Age oriels. . . . So, with all the past and present pouring in me, I roll down my billow from afar.

On one occasion King Media upbraids Babbalanja for habitually quoting an ancient poet, Bardianna. Babbalanja retorts that it is not so much a case of his quoting Bardianna, as of Bardianna's having quoted the later-born Babbalanja. If there is any difficulty in grasping Babbalanja's meaning, he himself amplifies his theme in the later statement:

> We are full of ghosts and spirits. . . . And all our dead sires, verily, are in us; *that* is their immortality. From sire to son, we go on multiplying corpses in ourselves; for all of which are resurrections. Every thought's a soul of some past poet, hero, sage. We are fuller than a city.[15]

*Mardi* was first published in March, 1849, and in that month Melville wrote to Duyckinck,

> Lay it down that had not Sir Thomas Browne lived, Emerson would not have mystified—I will answer that had not Old Zack's father begot him, Old Zack would never have been the hero of Palo Alto. The truth is that we are all sons, grandsons, or nephews or great-nephews of those who go before us. No one is his own sire.[16]

Even in *Pierre* Melville spoke of Shakespeare in very similar terms, stating that *Hamlet* "is but Egyptian Memnon, Montaignised and modernised; for being but a mortal man Shakespeare had his fathers too."[17]

Finally, Melville wrote in *Redburn* that sailors making spun yarn "use odds and ends of old rigging called '*junk*,' the yarns of which are picked to pieces, and then twisted into new combinations, something as most books are manufactured."[18] Nor was Melville appreciably more facetious here than in the quotation last given from *Mardi*. He was merely generalizing on a process which can be seen at work even in one of his last manuscripts, that of *Billy Budd*. The story contains this sentence:

Their captain's announcement was listened to by the throng of standing sailors in a dumbness like that of a seated congregation of believers in Hell listening to their clergyman's announcement of his Calvinistic text.

At this point in the manuscript Melville wrote in brackets, "Jonathan Edwards," identifying this New England divine as the original for the clergyman in the quotation.[19] Probably Melville had in mind similarly definite literary or historical backgrounds for other passages which appear to have no certain sources. Scholarly studies, including the present one, may put some names in brackets where Melville may have placed them on manuscripts now lost, or did not do so because of unconcern, or could not do so because of unawareness or forgetfulness. In any event, Melville clearly recognized that most books, including his own, were conditioned by their authors' reading, and that the originality of man is not comparable in degree to that of God.

In the light of Melville's declaration of literary independence in *Pierre*, it should not be surprising if this study reveals fewer direct traces of Milton in *Pierre* than in some other of Melville's works. In the particular light of the statement that "no one *great* book must ever be separately regarded," it should not be surprising if this study reveals no instances of such spectacular shoplifting as have been revealed in Melville's use of L'Estrange and of Nathaniel Ames,[20] but instead deals primarily with matters of style and characterization, with a lifelong and pervasive indebtedness rather than with random thefts. And in the final light of all the passages quoted above from *Pierre, Mardi, Redburn,* and *Billy Budd*, it would indeed be surprising if the examination of Melville's literary sires had produced no valuable fruit already, and should produce no more in the near future. Melville himself has authorized this study.

That Melville read widely and was influenced by his reading was a result of the kinds of books he wrote and of the way in which his art developed. That Milton should be one—and a major one—of the authors whom he read and by whom he was influenced, was a result of the nature of his environment and of the cast of his mind.

For present purposes one of the most important elements of Melville's environment was Milton's popularity in America during

7

the first half of the nineteenth century. That popularity can be measured by various kinds of evidence.[21] Students of colonial America emphasize a constant growth of Milton's reputation and influence during the eighteenth century. Bibliographers list over sixty editions of his poems published in America between 1787 and 1851. Author after author of the half-century before the Civil War was clearly influenced by Milton—Irving, Poe, Margaret Fuller, Lowell, Emerson are typical. New England school children used *Paradise Lost* as a textbook. Sunday-school pupils and child-poets alike enjoyed Milton before they reached their teens. William Macready was expressing a contemporary truth, not making a prediction, when in 1852 he wrote that for those who seek beauty, "the majestic verse of Milton will become the instructive entertainment of the humblest hearth, and the children of its family will cluster round to listen, for improvement and sober pleasure, to the music of his 'mighty line.' "[22]

Certainly Melville as a child was not deprived of the improvement and sober pleasure promised from Milton. To begin with, there exists a mutilated copy of one of Melville's own schoolbooks, Lindley Murray's *English Reader*, designed "to improve youth in the art of reading; to meliorate their . . . language and sentiments; and to inculcate some of the most important principles of piety and virtue." Throughout the *Reader* is a total of two hundred and three lines from *Paradise Lost*.[23]

The *English Reader* Melville probably used at the Albany Academy; about *The London Carcanet, Containing Select Passages from the Most Distinguished Writers* we can be more certain. Presented to Melville as a prize for work done at the Academy, the volume prints not only three brief quotations from *Paradise Lost* and one from *Paradise Regained*, but also this sentimental sign of the times:

## WRITTEN IN A LADY'S 'MILTON.'

With virtue strong as yours had Eve been arm'd,
In vain the fruit had blush'd, or serpent charm'd;
Nor had our bliss by penitence been bought:—
Nor had frail Adam fell—nor Milton wrote.[24]

8

Melville's father and mother and brothers and sisters, sincerely and pervasively God-fearing, maintained in their home a strongly religious atmosphere where Milton must have been honored.[25] There exists, for example, a copy of Mrs. Chapone's *Letters on the Improvement of the Mind* which Allan Melville, Herman's father, gave to the novelist's mother-to-be, Maria Gansevoort. In the letter "On Politeness and Accomplishments" Mrs. Chapone particularly endorses the reading of "those immortal ornaments of our nation, *Shakespeare* and *Milton*. . . . Our great English poet, Milton, is as far above my praise as his *Paradise Lost* is above anything which I am able to read, except the sacred writers."[26] These statements gain increased significance from the fact that each was emphasized by marginal pencil lines drawn by some member of Melville's family.

When Melville grew to man's estate, he continued to find Milton a part of his environment. It was probably in 1848 that Melville's father-in-law, Lemuel Shaw, gave Elizabeth Shaw Melville the complete works of William Ellery Channing. The first essay of the first volume was Channing's "Remarks on the Character and Writings of John Milton." Channing praises Milton as a "sainted spirit . . . endowed with gifts of the soul, which have been imparted to few of our race, and conscious of having consecrated them through life to God and mankind. . . . We venerate him as a man of genius, but still more as a man of magnanimity and Christian virtue, who regarded genius and poetry as sacred gifts."[27] These quotations and numerous similar ones by Emerson lend conviction to F.O.Matthiessen's remark that in the time of Emerson and Channing, Milton "still remained the archetype of the poet for New England."[28] He was the archetype of the poet for Melville's wife too, as appears from her having written, in connection with difficulty in marketing Melville's first collection of verse, "I suppose that if John Milton were to offer 'Paradise Lost' to the Harpers tomorrow, it would be promptly rejected as 'unsuitable,' not to say denounced as dull."[29]

Yet Melville's friends probably knew Milton even better than did his relatives. J. B. Auld, whom Melville met through Evert Duyckinck, wrote that Nathaniel Parker Willis's "curls stick out like 'some bush with frizzled hair implicit,' "[30] handling the un-

9

familiar line from *Paradise Lost* as though it were a matter of course. Auld, Duyckinck, and Charles Fenno Hoffman, all friends of Melville, praised Milton in the periodicals which they edited and which Melville not only wrote for but read.[31] And Evert Duyckinck gave a further measure of his fondness for Milton by ultimately acquiring thirty editions of his prose and poetry—more than fifty volumes—in addition to several books about Milton.[32] All these were, of course, available to Melville for consultation and borrowing, as were the eleven editions of Milton's prose and poetry owned in 1850 by the New York Society Library.[33]

Other than Evert Duyckinck, the only important literary friend Melville seems to have had was Nathaniel Hawthorne. Although Duyckinck may have encouraged Melville to study *Paradise Lost*, it is Hawthorne with whom Melville is likely to have discussed its contents and form, for the friendships were different. That with Duyckinck seems to have been based on a common interest in the writing, publishing, and reading of books ancient and contemporary, whereas that with Hawthorne was built on their common concern with the fundamental problems of art and of man's moral life, and on their kinship of spirit. Hawthorne had studied Milton in his youth, and an understanding of *Paradise Lost* was subsequently of great importance in his developing a profound knowledge of the operation of evil in human nature.[34] Through his intimacy with Melville he may well have increased the latter's mature enjoyment and comprehension of Milton.

Melville found Milton also in books of travel, in music, and in the fine arts. When he read Parkman's *The California and Oregon Trail* and Cheever's *The Whale and His Captors*, he read of Milton's presence on the American land and sea frontiers.[35] He could have heard, in New York, performances of Haydn's *The Creation* and of Handel's *Samson*; both oratorios use librettos based on Milton, and both are mentioned in *White Jacket*.[36] Finally, Melville knew well at least one picture and one statue intended to illustrate lines by Milton. The former was a large wash drawing by John Martin, entitled *Satan Exalted Sat* and showing Satan in glory above his peers. (A reproduction forms the frontispiece of this volume.) This illustration of the opening lines of the second book of *Paradise Lost* hung several decades ago "over a sofa in the south wall

Hiram Powers, *Il Penseroso*

of the dining room at Arrowhead. If parts of an old newspaper still adhering to the back of the frame can be any guide, . . . [Melville] must have owned it in 1848."[37] If it was his by then, he may very well have placed it in Arrowhead when he moved there in 1850, and have left it in its place when he sold the Berkshire farm to his brother Allan in 1863.[38]

As for the work of sculpture, in March 1857 Melville visited the Florentine studio of the very popular American sculptor, Hiram Powers, and noted in his journal, "His America. Il Penseroso, Fisher Boy."[39] Of these the second, which had been finished in 1856, was fully costumed according to the details of Milton's lines,

> Come, pensive Nun, devout and pure,
> Sober, stedfast, and demure,
> All in a robe of darkest grain,
> Flowing with majestick train,
> And sable stole of Cyprus lawn,
> Over thy decent shoulders drawn.
> Come, but keep thy wonted state,
> With even step, and musing gait;
> And looks commercing with the skies,
> Thy rapt soul sitting in thine eyes:
> There, held in holy passion still,
> Forget thyself to marble.[40]

His relatives, his friends, the books and the art of his day, all reminded Melville of Milton's importance. But in surveying the public, external factors which drew Melville towards Milton, we gain most by clearing our way to the more difficult question of what internal, subjective characteristics made Melville an interested and sympathetic reader of him. What inner affinity did the two men have? The question is not a new one: "Why out of the countless books and newspapers that a man reads, out of all the . . . [plays] he sees and anecdotes he hears, does he attend to, remember, and use in his creative work just the items that he does, and these only?"[41]

Yet at the beginning we must recognize that apart from those intimately connected with certain characters or traits of style, there are few ideas which Melville clearly owed to Milton. At least three explanations for such a situation can be offered: that most of the ideas of Melville the novelist and of Milton the poet are identi-

11

fied with some character or other; that their contrasting intellectual environments prevented overmuch congeniality in some important realms of speculation; and that the ancestries of mutually held ideas such as that of the fall of man are not always certain.[42] The first of these points will be illustrated in two of the following chapters. The second can be illustrated from a quotation: Milton's theology did not speak to the condition of the man who wrote that the young soul

> clamours for the support of its mother the world, and its father the Diety. But it shall yet learn to stand independent, though not without many a bitter wail, and many a miserable fall.[43]

The third explanation may be illustrated by Merton Sealts's admission that the source of Melville's doctrine of the indestructibility of evil was either Plato, Neoplatonism, Gnosticism, Milton, Spinoza, Goethe, or some other influence.[44] Only when similar ideas are expressed in similar words is there ground for suspecting indebtedness, as in both authors' statements that man's speculation is circular. In checking Adam's curiosity about matters astronomical, Raphael points out the vanity of trying to solve God's mysteries by means of

> Cycle and epicycle, orb in orb.[45]

Quoting from a chapter which Bardianna had entitled

> Cycles and Epicycles, with Notes on the Ecliptic,

Babbalanja ridicules man's "perpetual cycling . . . without progression."[46] Although they probably do not represent Melville's considered opinion, there are elsewhere in *Mardi* and in its companion works repeated statements of the same Miltonic tenor, akin to Raphael's advice:

> Sollicit not thy thoughts with matters hid;
> Leave them to God above; him serve, and fear![47]

We should also recognize that some characteristics of Milton must have repelled Melville. Milton's belief that most theological and philosophical queries were susceptible of abiding, Christian answers ran counter to Melville's indecisiveness and essential agnosticism. Nor did Milton show so strong a sense of humor as

12

Melville's, nor so luxuriant a symbolism. These differences, however, must have meant less to Melville than did his affinities to Milton.

Probably Melville never subjected Milton's ideas or style to any systematic scrutiny. Like Emerson, who found in reading not fresh ideas but a vocabulary for his own thoughts,[48] Melville seems to have read more for substantiation of his own opinions than for any planned disciplining of his mind. As he wrote of his own Captain Vere, "in this love of reading he found confirmation of his own more reserved thoughts—confirmation which he had vainly sought in social converse."[49] The proof of Melville's reading habits lies in the markings which he made in the extant volumes of his library. Chosen from many possible examples, there is this passage from Chatterton's "Happiness":

> Priestcraft! thou universal blind of all,
> Thou idol, at whose feet all nations fall;
> Father of misery, origin of sin,
> Whose first existence did with fear begin;
> Still sparing deal thy seeming blessings out,
> Veil thy Elysium with a cloud of doubt.

In the margin by these couplets Melville drew a pencil line some time between December 1849 and January 1854.[50] Whoever has read his earlier expressions of the same attitude, particularly in the Maramma chapters of *Mardi*, will probably conclude that Melville was indicating delight not in the perception of an idea fresh to him, but delight in finding his own views in another's book. They were, be it observed, views which he might vainly seek to have confirmed in social converse. And since Melville did read for confirmation, a large part of the reason for his reading Milton carefully must lie in those of his own conceptions which Milton could confirm. In what broad sweeps of the mind, then, were the two authors alike?

The material which has just been used to show that Melville read for confirmation of his own thought might lead to the conclusion that Christian Milton and Agnostic Melville had little in common. Such a conclusion would actually be false. In the first place, Melville drew his line beside an attack on priestcraft, not on religion; Milton had attacked priestcraft repeatedly. In the second place, the two authors were united by something more important

13

than holding common decisions about religion; they used identical ways of reaching those decisions.

Milton, living in that period of English history when sectarian quarrels were probably at high-water mark, reacted to the differences which surrounded him by facing all the issues squarely, honestly, and learnedly. The result of his thinking was a personal religion of combined individualism and tolerance—a religion in advance of most creeds or practices of his day, with the exception of Quakerism. Melville, living two centuries later, found himself in the midst of a struggle as intense as the earlier sectarian one— the struggle between traditional Christianity on the one hand, and science and the Higher Criticism on the other. Furthermore, Melville's firsthand observations of American Protestantism at home and abroad, of South Sea heathenism pristine and corrupted, and his published interpretations of the observed contrasts made him a principal in the early skirmishes of a sectarian struggle which was to broaden until it formed the intellectual background of *Clarel*. Melville's reactions in the face of so many disputes were precisely what Milton's had been—independence, reflection, open-mindedness. And also like Milton, Melville reached a creed of individualism and of toleration more acceptable to us than to his contemporaries. Where the toleration of both men weakened was in the matter of Roman Catholicism, which they together scorned, as, in Melville's symbolism, seamen always scorn those who "craven crawl to land."[51] The ultimate difference in the two creeds was that whereas the surge of Milton's century had carried him beyond all sects but not beyond the Church, the tide of Melville's era bore him beyond the Church itself. But the propelling spirits were the same. And the worldly results were much the same too. In his disappointment and depression after 1849, Melville could discover a personal kinship with the Milton who had found his genius also "fallen on evil days . . . and evil tongues."[52]

But "however quickly the young Herman threw off the orthodoxy which descended to him from both sides of the family, two marks of it remained, a minute knowledge of the Bible and a speculative interest in the central problem of Calvinism, the freedom of the will."[53] The same marks help to identify John Milton. His knowledge of the Bible served as a foundation for almost all

14

his works, while it is freedom of the will which justifies God's ways to man in both *Paradise Lost* and *Samson Agonistes*. The fascination of this problem for Melville, and Hawthorne's picture of him reasoning "as he always does, . . . of Providence and futurity, and of everything that lies beyond human ken,"[54] inevitably suggest a parallel with Milton and his description of the fallen angels who

> reason'd high
> Of providence, foreknowledge, will, and fate;
> Fix'd fate, free will, foreknowledge absolute;
> And found no end, in wandering mazes lost.[55]

But we have not only Hawthorne's description of Melville; we have also Melville's analysis of his contemporary. This analysis is valuable here because in the following paragraph, as elsewhere,[56] though his ostensible subject is Hawthorne, Melville actually describes himself. Consequently, he reveals one source of his own interest in Milton when he appears to uncover only Hawthorne's kinship with authors like the poet:

> Whether Hawthorne has simply availed himself of . . . mystical blackness as a means to the wondrous effects he makes it to produce in his lights and shades; or whether there really lurks in him, perhaps unknown to himself, a touch of Puritanic gloom,—this, I cannot altogether tell. Certain it is, however, that this great power of blackness in him derives its force from its appeals to that Calvinistic sense of Innate Depravity and Original Sin, from whose visitations, in some shape or other, no deeply thinking mind is always and wholly free. For, in certain moods, no man can weigh this world without throwing in something, somehow like Original Sin, to strike the uneven balance.[57]

This passage assumes even more significance in the light of what has been said earlier of Hawthorne's knowledge of Milton and friendship with Melville. Probably Melville could have said with a meaning more limited than that which he actually intended, "This Hawthorne has dropped germinous seeds into my soul."[58] *Paradise Lost* and other of Milton's works very likely attracted both Americans because of the large concern of all three authors with the origins, workings, and powers of evil. We know that Melville found fault with Emerson for failing to attach sufficient importance to evil;[59] he could not accuse Milton of denying the devil his due. Reared in an era of transcendental-religious optimism, Melville found himself alienate from that mood, and closer to

15

the much more measured optimism of Hawthorne and of Milton. Milton, Hawthorne, and Melville pondered the problem of evil in order, if possible, to assert the justice of God's ways. And Melville and Milton had surprisingly congruous visions of what the world would be if man had not introduced wrong to adulterate God's ways; one expressed it in his first work, the other in his greatest. William Ellery Sedgwick summarizes in the following fashion Melville's vision as embodied in *Typee*:

> What Melville is finally expressing in *Typee* is an inward and universal phase of human experience, obtaining in individuals and peoples alike;—the phase in which life lies along the easy slopes of spontaneous, instinctive being, in which human consciousness is a simple and happy undertaking of rudimentary sensations and simple sensuous impressions; in which physical health and good animal spirits have a large preponderance; in which the impulses and affections of the human heart suffer no disguise nor any distortion; the phase, finally, in which as yet no painful cleavage is felt dividing a happy animality from the gentlest and most guileless impulses of the heart.[60]

This is remarkably similar to what Paul Elmer More found to be the theme of *Paradise Lost*:

> The true theme [of *Paradise Lost*] is Paradise itself; not Paradise lost, but the reality of that "happy rural seat". . . . It is the good fortune of English literature that the Hebraic preoccupation of her epic poet led him to adopt a theme whose origin is that ancient ineradicable longing of the human heart for a garden of innocence, a paradise of idyllic delights, a region to which come only "golden days fruitful of golden deeds."[61]

Yet perhaps the emphasis should be shifted somewhat. After all, the ruling conscious interests of both men lay not in a Paradise either of Eden or of Typee, but in the noblest potentialities of fallen, finite man. Moreover, the man in whom they were interested was not only fallen and finite man; he was common man. "In the long invocation to the ninth book [of *Paradise Lost*] Milton repudiates the pomp and circumstance of traditional epics for the more truly heroic and tragic theme of human sin."[62] And in his novels Melville renounces the pomp and circumstance of public grandeur to write of an unknown Yankee Jackson who can be matched with Tiberius, and of a Billy Budd who meets profoundest passion on a scrubbed gundeck. In *Moby-Dick* Melville found "all outward majestical trappings and housings"[63] denied him, even as

16

Milton had found himself denied "Bases and tinsel Trappings, gorgeous Knights."[64] "Oh, Ahab! what shall be grand in thee, it must needs be plucked at from the skies, and dived for in the deep, and featured in the unbodied air!"

Throughout all his mature years Melville must have enjoyed the Milton who attacked priestcraft, who accepted God and the church on his own terms only, who was preoccupied with the conflict between good and evil, who had almost a Polynesian concept of man's ideal life, and who for epic literature did not need aristocratic trappings. There was also for his enjoyment the Milton who was a fellow champion of intellectual and civil liberty, a brother patriot who loved his country enough to criticize it harshly, another mind which insisted on finding its own truths, which delighted in "deep earnest thinking, . . . the intrepid effort of the soul to keep the open independence of her sea." Finally, Melville recognized that "to produce a mighty book, you must choose a mighty theme."[65] He could have been describing *Paradise Lost* when he wrote that "most grand productions of the best human intellects ever are built round a circle, . . . digestively including the whole range of all that can be known or dreamed."[66] And Melville preferred not only to write all-inclusive books, but to read them too. Milton's works met the specifications. "Not for nothing one face, one character, one fact, makes much impression on him, and another none. This sculpture in the memory is not without pre-established harmony."[67]

17

# CHAPTER TWO

# THE INFLUENCE
# OF MILTON'S MINOR WORKS

> *"I have endeavoured to shew
> how the Genius of the Poet
> shines by a happy Invention,
> a distant Allusion, or a
> judicious Imitation."*
> —*Addison on* Paradise Lost *in
> the* Spectator, *No. CCCLXIX.*

THE statements which other scholars have heretofore made about Milton's influence on Melville fall generally into three classes. In the first of these is a rather small number of scattered, parenthetical notations of some of Melville's more obvious echoes of Milton. Typical of the group is the information that Melville

made numerous references to Milton; and he significantly marked passages in his copy of Shelley's *Essays* which relate to anti-Christian argument in *Paradise Lost.*

To that a note adds:

*Mardi,* I, 344; II, 241; *Redburn,* pp. 244, 324, 356; *White-Jacket,* p. 35, etc.; and see Melville's copy of Shelley's *Essays,* . . . I, 33.[1]

Such statements may not be very stimulating, but they are at least precise and easily proved. Statements of the second class are stimulating and precise, but not easily proved: Melville "could write with . . . the grandeur of Milton."[2] Statements of the third class appear to be neither precise nor stimulating, and either in no need of proof or incapable of proof. Fair samples are these:

With Melville, the English romantic period occupies only a subordinate position in comparison to that of the Renaissance; it provides him with no prototypes even approximately as powerful as Shakespeare, Rabelais, or Milton.[3]

18

Much of . . . [Melville's] knowledge [of the Bible] must have come from church attendance, some pictorially, and some through intermediate sources, such as Bunyan, Browne, and Milton.[4]

All three types of statement suggest the difficulties which beset most studies of influence—how are the skeins to be unraveled? Did Melville twice mention Urim and Thummim[5] because *Paradise Lost* and *Paradise Regained* had impressed them on his mind, or because he recalled them from the Bible, or because of some other influence? How far should the sails of speculation be spread? How much ballast of minute facts can be taken aboard before the weight of the ballast becomes dead weight? Clearly we are always between a Scylla and a Charybdis.

In the present work, as we turn to the actual effect and moment-to-moment cause of Milton's influence on Melville we shall banish to Appendix B much of the ballast of fact, and shall loosen our sails chiefly to those speculations which seem most clearly author-ized by facts and which are most important to the processes of Melville's art. In other words, trying to avoid both the boringly insignificant and the hopelessly indefinite, we shall survey the major borrowings that Melville assuredly or probably made from Milton, and we shall try to keep in mind the very important questions of why he used what he did, and of how he used it. We shall approach these purposes first through Melville's use of Milton's life, his prose, and his poetry other than *Paradise Lost*, for in this limited area we can examine carefully certain habits which we shall find operating more complexly and more actively in Melville's use of *Paradise Lost*.

Melville gives no evidence of having known a great deal about Milton's life, partly because in Melville's day less was known about Milton than is known now, and partly because Melville was not much interested in biography. But he did know that Milton had been in Italy and that he had become blind, though of only the latter fact did he make any use that could be called significant.[6]

This use of Milton's blindness was made in two works published in 1849. *Redburn*, the later of the two, contains a description of a blind beggar of Liverpool:

This old man sang, or rather chanted, certain words in a peculiarly long-drawn,

19

guttural manner, throwing back his head, and turning up his sightless eyeballs
to the sky. His chant was a lamentation upon his infirmity; and at the time it
produced the same effect upon me that my first reading of Milton's "Invocation
to the Sun" did, years afterward. I cannot recall it all; but it was something like
this, drawn out in an endless groan:—
  "Here goes the blind old man; blind, blind, blind; no more will he see sun nor
moon—no more see sun nor moon!"[7]

When Melville wrote this passage, his experiences in Liverpool
were twelve years behind him. That interval of itself might suggest that the opening lines of Book III of *Paradise Lost*, in which
Milton hails the sun and laments his blindness, were the real source
of Melville's entire passage. But there is the further fact that
whereas specific scenes of Liverpool were far back in Melville's
memory, Milton's blindness was fresh in his mind. He had just
written in *Mardi*, "Blind Milton sings bass to my Petrarchs and
Priors," and almost three hundred pages later in *Mardi* occurs this
relevant dialogue:

At last, we talked of old Homeric bards:—those who, ages back, harped, and
begged, and groped their blinded way through all this charitable . . . [world];
receiving coppers then, and immortal glory now.
ABRAZZA.—How came it, that they all were blind?
BABBALANJA.—It was endemical, your highness. Few grand poets have good
eyes; for they needs blind must be, who ever gaze upon the sun.[8]

Although Milton is not mentioned in this dialogue, he was almost
surely one of the "Homeric bards," for his life and the references
to him in *Redburn* and *Mardi* all lead to that conclusion. Furthermore, some of Milton's lines may well have suggested the whole
theme of the Homeric bards' being blind:

nor [do I] sometimes forget
Those other two equall'd with me in fate,
So were I equall'd with them in renown,
Blind Thamyris, and blind Mæonides,
And Tiresias, and Phineus, prophets old.[9]

This passage is from the very "Invocation to the Sun" mentioned
in *Redburn*, and notes commenting upon it could have told Melville
what he perhaps knew himself—more about Homer and of blindness: "Mæonides" was Homer's patronymic; Thamyris is mentioned in Homer's poem of Troy; Phineus was blinded by the sun.
Here were Homeric bards, their blindness, and the sun ready-

20

combined. Sun and poetry, blind Homeric bards and begging, seem then to have been associated around Melville's awareness of Milton's blindness and of its role in his poetry. And it seems not unlikely that this one fact about Milton's life claimed so much of Melville's attention because his own eyesight was beginning to fail him, and because he may have feared that constant application of his eyes would blind him as it had blinded Milton. Only three years after *Redburn*, when he wrote of Pierre's attempt at authorship, Melville made virtual loss of sight one of his character's crowning calamities. By then his own sight was worse, not better. Perhaps in blindness we have another link of inner affinity between the two authors.

Melville seems to have known Milton's prose hardly better than his life; the scanty evidence continues to come from the late 1840's. Referring to England by an allegorical name, Melville observed in *Mardi* that

> time was, when Dominora was republican, down to her sturdy backbone. The son of an absolute monarch became the man Karolus; and his crown and head both rolled in the dust. And Dominora had her patriots by thousands; and lusty Defences and glorious Areopagiticas were written, not since surpassed; and no turban was doffed save in homage of . . . [God].[10]

These references to Milton's *Areopagitica* and to his first and second defenses of the English people help to make the allegory of Dominora both full and identifiable. Yet neither this passage nor any other gives proof that Melville knew more than the titles and occasions of these three of Milton's prose works.[11] Nevertheless, all the information in the quotation might have been derived from *Areopagitica* and the defenses of the English people, the latter of which were lusty in the sense of being at times obscene as well as in the sense of being usually vigorous.

There is additional reason for believing that Melville had read at least *Areopagitica*. The theme in *Pierre* that "only by being guilty of Folly does mortal man in many cases arrive at the perception of Sense"[12] is reminiscent of Milton's emphasis on the necessity of training oneself in virtue:

> What wisdom can there be to choose, what continence to forbear, without the knowledge of evil? . . . Therefore the knowledge and survey of vice is in this

21

world so necessary to the constituting of human virtue, and the scanning of error to the confirmation of truth.

Much more significant, however, are Melville's echoes of the analogy in *Areopagitica* of books to men. "Books are not absolutely dead things," Milton wrote,

> but do contain a progeny of life in them to be as active as that soul was whose progeny they are; nay, they do preserve as in a vial the purest efficacy and extraction of that living intellect that bred them, ... and being sown up and down, may chance to spring up armed men. ... A good book is the precious lifeblood of a master spirit, imbalmed and treasured up on purpose to a life beyond life.[13]

In reviewing Cooper's *The Red Rover*, Melville employed this idea, giving it a humorous twist not only to create humor for its own sake, but also to use that humor as an effective method of driving home an idea—that the binding of a book should correspond to the character of the book:

> Books, gentlemen, are a species of men, and introduced to them you circulate in the "very best society" that this world can furnish, without the intolerable infliction of "dressing" to go into it. ... Men, then, that they are ... books should be appropriately apparelled.[14]

In *Clarel* the comparison reappears in the question,

> Were it a paradox to confess
> A book's a man?[15]

In these possible influences of *Areopagitica* we are, however, merely moving from a known Miltonic reference to a suggested Miltonic echo. The process is somewhat like that necessary in the preceding discussion of Melville's use of Milton's blindness, but with a difference. The theme of blindness ran through that discussion; in this, we were forced to move from the title of a work to an idea in that work.

Fortunately we can deal in other instances with quotations. The only other prose work by Milton which Melville appears to have known is *Of Education.* "Were you ever homeward bound?" asks White Jacket.

> Fly to the uttermost parts of the earth. There, tarry a year or two; and then let the gruffest of boatswains, his lungs all goose-skin, shout forth those magical words, ["All hands up anchor! We're homeward bound!"] and you'll swear *"the harp of Orpheus were not more enchanting."*[16]

22

Here for the first time we meet what will eventually appear to be the rule rather than an exception—a phrase quoted by a memory which played strange tricks. What Melville's mind began with was Milton's prophecy,

> I will point out the right path of a virtuous and noble education; . . . so full of goodly prospect, and melodious sounds on every side, that *the harp of Orpheus was not more charming.*[17]

Over-enthusiasm for the subjunctive mood, or a tasteful preference for liquids to sibilants may have caused Melville's substitution of *were* for *was*. But what caused his introduction of *enchanting* for *charming?* For one matter, Milton's wording has a less pleasant rhythm than the regular iambic stress of Melville's. A second factor may have been Melville's recollection of the question in "Lycidas,"

> What could the Muse herself that *Orpheus* bore,
> The Muse herself, for her *enchanting* son?[18]

Orpheus' name in *Of Education* presumably attracted to itself the adjective linked with it in "Lycidas." The shift was a simple associational transfer, which John Livingston Lowes would have explained in terms of hooked atoms operating in the deep well of the unconscious.[19]

What was revealed by this examination of a quotation from *Of Education* should teach us to be wary: Melville's use of quotation marks may aid us by indicating an indebtedness, but they may not tell us the full story of that indebtedness. The quotation marks may point out merely the first clue of a previously unsuspected trait of Melville's mind. This generalization can be further demonstrated by two quotations from "L'Allegro."

This poem provided one of the choice selections of divine poesy with which Melville ostentatiously speckled his juvenile "Fragments From a Writing-Desk." The author prays, "Waft me, ye gentle gales, beyond this lower world and,

> 'Lap me in soft Lydian airs!' "[20]

Another quotation from "L'Allegro,"

> Haste thee, Nymph, and bring with thee . . .
> *Quips, and Cranks,* and wanton Wiles,
> Nods, and Becks, *and wreathed Smiles,*[21]

23

served Melville's purposes while he was reviewing two books of the sea for *The Literary World*. In his altered version, we are told, concerning a certain captain, that when once at sea

his Nautical Highness left behind him all his *"Quips and cranks and wreathed smiles."*[22]

Here again, as in the borrowing from "Lycidas" used to alter the quotation from *Of Education*, Melville's memory may have misled him, but within the bounds of Miltonism. In both instances Milton is used to adulterate Milton. It seems more likely in this case, however, that Melville purposely sacrificed the alliteration as well as the fidelity of "wanton Wiles." He was using the quotation to describe the prepossessing shore habits of a captain, and "wreathed Smiles" fitted that purpose whereas "wanton Wiles" did not. Curiously enough, the first half of *"Nods, and Becks*, and wreathed Smiles" was not wasted in Melville's memory, for the congregation of "The Two Temples" leaves church "in three freshets—all gay, sprightly *nods and becks."*[23]

But Melville is not always so helpful as to mark his borrowings with quotation marks. There is, for example, this passage from "The Encantadas":

Selfish ambition, or the love of rule for its own sake, far from being the peculiar *infirmity of noble minds*, is shared by beings which have no minds at all.[24]

Clearly Melville is repeating part of a familiar quotation from "Lycidas":

Fame is the spur that the clear spirit doth raise
(That last *infirmity of noble mind*).[25]

Or consider the statements in *Moby-Dick* that whales are

*most monstrous* and *most mountainous*,

and that the *Pequod* was

a noble craft, but somehow a *most melancholy*.[26]

Taken separately, neither quotation would seem unusual, but when one notices that they are separated by only eight pages of text, and when one recalls Milton's description of Philomel as

Most musical, most melancholy,[27]

24

one more than suspects that Melville consciously parodied Milton in his statement about whales, and consciously echoed him in referring to the *Pequod.*

A hidden echo or quotation of this sort is almost indistinguishable from other passages where the indebtedness for words and images is perhaps less clearly demonstrable but none the less probable. For example, F. O. Matthiessen has observed that Melville's " 'A Requiem for Soldiers Lost in Ocean Transports' . . . seems to echo 'Lycidas' in some of its undersea images,"[28] probably intending a comparison between the following lines: *Lycide.*

> Melville: . . . Save them that by the *fabled shore,*
> *Down the* pale *stream* are *washed away.*
> *Far* to the reef of *bones are* borne;
> And never revisits them the light.[29]

> Milton: His goary visage *down the stream* was sent,
> *Down the* swift Hebrus to the Lesbian *shore*
> . . . . . . . . . . . . . . . . . . . . . . . . . . . . . . .
> Whilst thee the *shores* and sounding seas
> *Wash far away,* where'er thy *bones are* hurl'd,
> Whether beyond the stormy Hebrides,
> Where thou perhaps, under the whelming tide,
> Visit'st the bottom of the monstrous world;
> Or whether thou, to our moist vows denied,
> Sleep'st by the *fable* of Bellerus old.[30]

It is obvious that more fables than that of Bellerus are active in Milton's lines and could have suggested Melville's "fabled," which has little other *raison d'être* in his poem. It is equally obvious that the italics in the passages can indicate only specific verbal repetitions. Additional general resemblances, as of corpses drifting to strange and unpleasant places, can, I believe, be left to the reader's own perception.

A further key to Melville's debt to Milton's minor poems lies in references such as that which Melville made in thanking George Duyckinck for Chapman's Homer:

As for Pope's version . . . I expect it,—when I shall put Chapman's beside it— to go off *shrieking,* like the bankrupt deities in Milton's hymn.[31]

The hymn referred to, from Milton's "On the Morning of Christ's Nativity," describes exiled Apollo leaving Delphos with a "hollow *shriek.*" A second exiled deity, Ashtaroth, is mentioned in *Clarel*,[32] and a third, Moloch, supplied Melville with a vivid analogy which will be discussed at the end of Chapter V. ✓

References to Milton's life and works, acknowledged and un-acknowledged quotations, verbal echoes—all these can set one on the trail of Milton's influence on Melville. One final kind of clue remains to be discussed in terms of Milton's minor poems. That kind is the rhythms of Melville's prose.

Not long after *Moby-Dick*, there appeared Melville's "The Paradise of Bachelors," which contains this sentence:

> In mild meditation pace the cloisters; *take your pleasure, sip your leisure, in the garden waterward*; go linger in the ancient library; go worship in the sculptured chapel.[33]

In the italicized words is one of those occasional melodies which lie haphazardly latent for the delight of the careful reader of Melville's prose. In this case of what was probably premeditated verse, Milton seems to have inspired the rhythm. One reason for the latter presumption is that this rhythm of Melville's prose can be duplicated in some of the lines of "Il Penseroso." A second reason is that Melville's words as well as his rhythm have a Miltonic strain. Let us reset Melville and quote Milton:

> *Take* your *pleasure*, sip your *leisure*,
> *In* the *garden* waterward.

> And add to these retired *Leisure*,
> That *in* trim *gardens takes* his *pleasure*.[34]

The foregoing discussion of Melville's most important uses of Milton's life, prose works, and minor poetry is in no sense an indication of the depth of Melville's debt to Milton.[35] That debt was contracted, in all its most significant parts, from *Paradise Lost*. The foregoing discussion does, however, not only illustrate many types of evidence which will be handled in the rest of the present study, but it also accomplishes other ends.

For one thing, it gives a part of the evidence which will ultimately demonstrate that Melville knew some of Milton's works intimately, that we need be in no doubt of the existence of a knowledge which could lead to an influence. In the second place, it gives evidence that those of Milton's works which Melville seems to have known best are those most likely to be best-known today—of the prose, *Areopagitica* and *Of Education*; of the minor poems, "Lycidas," "L'Allegro," and "Il Penseroso." For another matter, it demonstrates that some borrowings, such as quotations and references, were conscious, that others, such as that from "Lycidas" for "A Requiem," were probably unconscious, and that between those extremes lies a *terra incognita* where one may endlessly, and probably fruitlessly, debate the consciousness of such a borrowing as "most melancholy" or the purposefulness of such a misquotation as "Quips and cranks and wreathed smiles."

Perhaps more important is the fact that the foregoing discussion provides a basis for preliminary conclusions about the effects which Melville achieved with his borrowings from Milton. Something has already been said about the effects achieved with some of the borrowings. One fairly obvious point should not, however, be overlooked: many of the effects depend on the amount of equipment in the reader's mind. All readers can recognize a quotation as a quotation when it is in quotation marks, as was "The harp of Orpheus were not more enchanting." Far fewer readers, however, can catch the rich connotations—or indeed see anything but a cliché—in the hidden quotation of "infirmity of noble minds." Similarly, any sensitive ear might find delight in the meter and rhyme of "take your pleasure, sip your leisure, in the garden water-ward." Only a mind of a certain training, however, would catch the full flavor of the statement that "when Dominora was republican . . . lusty Defences and glorious Areopagiticas were written, not since surpassed." Melville's knowledge of Milton provided one method by which he could shift from a less richly to a more richly connotative style, increasing the flow of concepts in his readers' minds. It enabled him to achieve special effects of humor, illustration, erudition, suggestiveness, and the like. He could achieve these effects by so revealing or even parading his borrowings as to leave the uninformed reader curious or perplexed by references he does not understand and quotations he cannot place. He could also achieve these effects while concealing his borrowings and so making them seem like inherent, inbred values of his style. Thus hidden, the borrowings would not embarrass readers who lacked proper training, and would give double delight to readers who possessed it. Proper training included a knowledge of Milton—of his minor works, but particularly of *Paradise Lost*.

# CHAPTER THREE

# MILTON'S INFLUENCE
# ON MELVILLE'S VOCABULARY
# AND SENTENCE STRUCTURE

> "*Since I have undertaken to man-handle
> this leviathan, it behooves me to
> approve myself omnisciently
> exhaustive in the enterprise.*"
> —Moby-Dick, *II, 219.*

Moby-Dick is a symphony; every resource of language
and thought, fantasy, description, philosophy, natural history, drama, broken rhythms, blank verse, imagery, symbol, are utilized to sustain and expand the great theme.[1]

Nor is this true of only one of Melville's works. The symphony
of *Moby-Dick* is composed of elements which appear in greater or
less degree throughout all Melville's writing; the style of *Moby-
Dick* is the style not of a book, but of a man, and "ceux de ses
livres qui restent vraiment grands vivent par le style autant que
par la pensée."[2] Only by examining each element of style in turn,
and wherever it appears in a most useful form, can we hope to
assay Milton's role in fashioning the total counterpoint. The
simplest element with which to begin, because the most definite, is
Melville's quotations from *Paradise Lost*. Even a mere listing of
these quotations is impressive.

In *Typee* Melville gave a touch of literary pretension to the
style of his first book by writing, in connection with the danger of
his being tattooed,

29

nothing but the utter ruin of my 'face divine,' as the poets call it, would . . .
satisfy the inexorable Mehevi.[3]

The plural *poets* suggests, of course, that Melville either had read
the quotation in several poets' works, or had forgotten its source
and wished to mask his ignorance behind a generality. "Face
divine" does appear in Spenser,[4] but its more probable source is in
*Paradise Lost*:

> Or flocks, or herds, or human *face divine*.[5]

In Melville's next work, *Omoo*, there is an exact transcription of
Milton's translation of Virgil's "Parvis componere magna":[6]

> The first rays of the morning . . . flashed into view at one end of the arched night,
> like—*to compare great things with small*—the gleamings of Guy Fawkes's lantern
> in the vaults of the Parliament House.[7]

But in *Redburn* an inexact quotation may give even better evidence
of Melville's familiarity with *Paradise Lost*, for it probably shows
that he thought he knew the poem well enough to quote it from
memory. He had read of Satan's legions that

> anon they move
> In perfect phalanx *to the Dorian mood*
> *Of flutes and soft recorders.*

What he wrote was that the *Irrawaddy's*

> cargo was discharged . . . '*to the sound of flutes and soft recorders.*'[8]

The discrepancy between "to the Dorian mood" and "to the
sound" might be explained in a number of ways. One explanation,
however, is closest both to Milton's poetry and to Melville's
practice in the compounding of "The harp of Orpheus were not
more enchanting." This explanation is that Melville took his cue
from a passage only a hundred and sixty lines later than that of
"the Dorian mood." Here Pandemonium rises

> with *the sound*
> *Of* dulcet symphonies.[9]

Perhaps this is how the *Irrawaddy's* cargo came to be discharged
"to *the sound of* flutes and soft recorders."

A second instance of Melville's using *Paradise Lost* with familiarity occurs in *Redburn* in a description of fog.

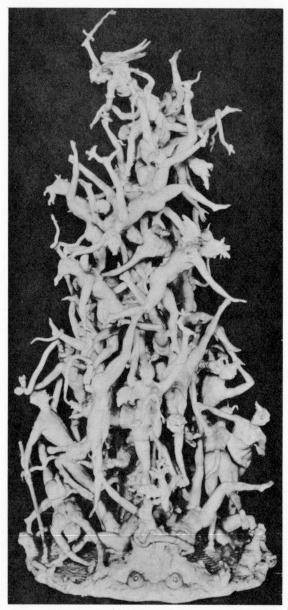

Agostino Fasolato, *La caduta degli angeli ribelli*

What is this that we sail through? What *palpable obscure?*

Beelzebub had asked,

> Who shall tempt with wandering feet
> The dark unbottom'd *infinite* abyss,
> And through the *palpable obscure* find out
> His uncouth way?[10]

*Infinite* is here italicized because it was used by Melville one year after *Redburn* in connection with an identical use of *obscure* as a noun:

> Blackness it is that furnishes the *infinite obscure* of . . . [Hawthorne's] background.[11]

Two quotations from *Paradise Lost*, one of three lines and the second of five, are among the "Extracts" which introduce readers to the narrative of *Moby-Dick*; the longer quotation appeared also on the title page of the first English edition of *The Whale*.[12] Five years after the publication of *Moby-Dick* in 1851, Melville adroitly and humorously slipped a passage from Milton's epic into financial talk aboard the devil-damned *Fidèle*. A confidence man says,

> There will be a reaction; from the stock's *descent* its *rise* will be higher *than from no fall*, the holders *trusting themselves to fear no second fate.*

But a yet greater deceiver, Satan, had told his dupes,

> From this *descent*
> Celestial virtues *rising*, will appear
> More glorious and more dread *than from no fall*,
> And *trust themselves to fear no second fate.*[13]

Not long thereafter Melville described a "fine morning, off 'Lemnos, the Ægean isle,' "[14] being familiar enough with *Paradise Lost* to quote these four words in the journal of his trip to the Holy Land when he probably did not have a text of the poem before him. Less than a year after his return from the Holy Land, Melville is reported to have described in a lecture

> a marble group representing Lucifer and his companions cast down from Heaven, cut out of a single block of marble, amidst which appeared the unbroken, defiant form of Satan, his whole body breathing *revenge*, and his attitude one *never to submit or yield.*[15]

31

It was probably Melville and not the reporter who introduced the phrase from Satan's first speech in *Paradise Lost:*

> And study of *revenge,* immortal hate,
> And courage *never to submit or yield.*[16]

During his last extended voyage, that to California, Melville read Chapman's Homer and in a pencil note to the *Iliad* quoted "Milton —'rose like an exhalation.' "[17] Finally, three decades later, in his posthumous *Billy Budd* he quoted Milton's "Pale ire, envy and despair."[18]

From this chronological survey of eleven quotations from *Paradise Lost,* two instances have been omitted because of their unusual interest. Through them we can observe a gradual transition from quotation to paraphrase and verbal echo, so that the process of artistic digestion, of movement from one kind of influence to another, becomes momentarily visible.

In the first case we must begin with Milton's lines,

> Now gentle gales
> Fanning their *odoriferous* wings dispense
> Native perfumes, and whisper whence they stole
> Those *balmy spoils. As* when to them who *sail*
> Beyond the Cape of Hope, and now are past
> Mozambick, off at sea north-east *winds blow*
> *Sabean odours* from the spicy *shore*
> Of *Araby the blest;* with such delay
> Well pleas'd they slack their course, and many a league
> Cheer'd with the grateful smell old Ocean smiles:
> So entertain'd those *odorous sweets* the Fiend.[19]

In *Mardi* Melville mentioned "zephyrs from *Araby the blest,*"[20] but the next year he used the passage much more significantly. On the *Neversink,* he wrote, after too much Eau de Cologne had been drunk by thirsty sailors,

> It was *as* if we were *sailing* by some *odoriferous shore,* in the vernal season of violets. *Sabæan odours!*
>
> 'For many a league,
> Cheered with the grateful smell, old Ocean smiled.'[21]

Two passages in the much later *Clarel* show that Melville had not forgotten this quotation and its original context. Perhaps here as elsewhere *Tartarus* was the spur which, because of its use in *Paradise Lost*, brought Miltonic phrases to his mind:

> 'Get thee away,
> Nor in such coals of *Tartarus* rake.'

> So Rolfe; and wide a casement threw.
> Aroma! and is this Judæa?
> Down the long gorge of Kedron *blew*
> A *balm* beyond the *sweet Sabæa*—
> An air *as* from Elysian grass;
> Such freshening redolence divine
> As mariners upon the brine
> Inhale, when barren beach they pass
> By night; a musk of wafted *spoil*
> From Nature's scent-bags in the soil,
> Not in her flowers; nor seems it known
> Even on the *shores* wherefrom 'tis *blown*.

> Thou mayst recall . . .
> We breathed the *balm-wind* from *Sabæa*.[22]

In the second instance of transition from quotation to probably unconscious adaptation we begin with Melville's *Journal of a Visit to London and the Continent*, 1849-1850. Here again, as in his journal for 1856, he would hardly have quoted Milton if he had not been very familiar with him. The first of two relevant entries was made during the east-bound trip:

> Last evening was very pleasant. Walked the deck with the German, Mr. Adler till a late hour, talking of 'Fixed Fate, Free-will, fore-knowledge absolute' etc.[23]

Three months later the line from *Paradise Lost* was still in Melville's mind, for his notes of the west-bound crossing of the Atlantic include mention of

> Conversations with the Colonel on *fixed fate* &c. during the passage.[24]

Less than two years later Melville wove part of Milton's line into the symphony of *Pierre*:

> But Pierre was not arguing *Fixed Fate* and *Free Will*, now; *Fixed Fate* and *Free Will* were arguing him, and *Fixed Fate* got the better in the debate.[25]

Finally, when we recall what immediately precedes the line in *Paradise Lost* which we have been considering, we find the probable source of two lines in a poem from *Timoleon*. In *Paradise Lost* the fallen angels

> *reason'd* high
> *Of* providence, foreknowledge, will, and *fate;*
> Fix'd *fate, free will, foreknowledge absolute.*

In "The Age of the Antonines,"

> The sting was not dreamed to be taken from death,
> No *Paradise* pledged or sought,
> But they *reasoned of fate* at the flowing feast.[26]

These two cases of assimilated quotations aptly pave the way for consideration of two phrases which Melville never used as quotations but which nevertheless constitute obvious debts to Milton.

When Paul the Apostle wrote to the Colossians he told them that by God

> were all things created, that are in heaven, and that are in earth, visible and invisible, whether they be *thrones, or dominions, or principalities, or powers.*[27]

Clearly this was in Melville's mind when he wrote in *Mardi*,

> Thus all generations are blended: and heaven and earth of one kin: the hierarchies of seraphs in the uttermost skies; the *thrones and principalities* in the zodiac.[28]

But, interestingly enough, on the two later occasions when Melville used the phrase in question, he used its Miltonic and not its Biblical form. For Milton too had read and used *Colossians*, making it the basis of three different lines. For him, *principalities* became *princedoms,* and *dominions* twice became *dominations*:

> Thrones, Princedoms, Powers, Dominions.
> Thrones, Dominations, Princedoms, Virtues, Powers.
> Thrones, and Powers,/Princedoms, and Dominations.[29]

The second of these lines is spoken twice by Satan, once by God, and once by Abdiel; the reader of *Paradise Lost* can hardly avoid remembering it. Melville's first use of his memory of it was in a letter to Evert Duyckinck thanking him for some gifts:

> But the cigars!—The oriental looking box! and the Antilles smell of them! And the four different *thrones & dominations* of bundles, all harmonizing together like the Iroquois.[30]

The second use of Milton's phrasing occurred in "The Encantadas":

As we still ascend from shelf to shelf, we find the tenants of the tower serially disposed in order of their magnitude:—gannets, black and speckled haglets, jays, sea-hens, sperm-whale-birds, gulls of all varieties:—*thrones, princedoms, powers, dominating* one above another in senatorial array.[31]

Melville's second debt of this type was to the fourth line from the close of the epic:

> *The world was all before them*, where to choose
> Their place of rest, and Providence their guide.[32]

A mere chronological listing is sufficient demonstration of the changes this line underwent, and of the deep impression it had made on Melville's mind:

The Watery World is All Before Them. (*Mardi*, I, 35)
Mardi lies all before us. (*Mardi*, I, 234)
His own world is full before him. (*Mardi*, II, 322)
The world was before me. (*Redburn*, p. 11)
The world is all before us. ("I and My Chimney," XIII, 279)
See, the land/Is all before thee. (*Clarel*, II, 191)

Somewhat less decisively Miltonic, but nevertheless very probably so, are twenty or more passages by Melville which employ short phrases found also in *Paradise Lost*. Only two can be given here. In the first, we move from Milton's twice-written "world of woe"[33] to Melville's "watery world of woe" in *Moby-Dick*, and then wonder whether he had been aware of paraphrasing Milton just four pages earlier in "the whirl of woe."[34] The other case involves Milton's address to Light at the beginning of Book III and Melville's poem about the desert sun, from *Timoleon*. The pentameters are, of course, Milton's:

> Hail, *holy Light*, offspring of Heaven first-born.
>          . . . *God* is light
> And never but in unapproached light
> Dwelt from eternity, dwelt then in thee,
> *Bright effluence* of *bright essence* increate.

> Holy, holy, *holy Light!*
> Immaterial incandescence,
> Of *God* the *effluence* of the *essence*,
> Shekinah intolerably *bright!*[35]

35

Numerous other phrases, few of them distinctively Miltonic, occur in both authors' works—"solitary way," "weal or woe," "swift destruction," "grisly king," "of endless date," "numbers without number," for example. To cite them all here could lead only to boredom; they are given at length in Appendix B. There they lend increased validity to the statement that through the symphony of Melville's prose ran harmonies from Milton's organ.

And curiously enough, over eighty years before this study of Miltonic echoes was begun, Melville himself noted a Miltonic anticipation in one of his favorite authors. When he read in Chapman's Homer of

> The great Greek come, *spher'd round with beams,*

Melville underlined the words in italics, put a check in the margin, and above it wrote "Milton."[36] He had noted the similarity to the poet's phrases "*Spher'd* in a radiant cloud," "Smear'd *round with* pitch," and "inwreath'd *with beams.*"[37] Melville knew Milton well enough to detect his phrases as well as to use them; students of Melville should know Milton just as well, it seems—witness those investigators of Melville who have made the mistake of transcribing his Miltonic "fore-knowledge absolute" as "free-knowledge absolute,"[38] and his Miltonic "thrones and dominations" as "thrones and denominations."[39] But *terrae incognitae* spread in everyone's mind, partly for a reason which Melville touched on in *Redburn*:

> It is really wonderful how many names there are in the world. . . .
> I wonder whether mankind could not get along without all these names, which keep increasing every day, and hour, and moment; till at last the very air will be full of them; and even in a great plain men will be breathing each other's breath, owing to the vast multitude of words they use that consume all the air, just as lamp-burners do gas. But people seem to have a great love for names; for to know a great many names seems to look like knowing a great many things; though I should be not surprised if there were a great many more names than things in the world.[40]

Melville himself drew on an unusually full stock of names—that is, words—some of which may have gained their place in his vocabulary because of their occurrence in Milton, others of which may have been formed on Miltonic models or used in Miltonic ways. In the following discussion of Melville's vocabulary, the truth about the several classes of words will lie somewhere between the fact that as distinctive traits of Melville's prose they give it a Miltonic flavor, and the hyperbole that he derived all of them directly from his reading of the poet. Where to place the finger of truth each reader will have to decide for himself. In so doing he should bear in mind that instead of considering the commonplace features of either author's style, the following discussion deals with some of the individualizing characteristics which distinguish their language from that of other men, and which, as individualizing characteristics in Milton, must have attracted Melville's attention as he read *Paradise Lost* and its companion works. These characteristics then remained in his mind available for imitation, to become earmarks of his own passages of heightened emotion.

It must, however, be understood from the beginning that not all the possible illustrations of particular points will be noted. It will be deemed sufficient to demonstrate, in the text and Appendix B, that closely parallel practices did exist in both authors.[41] In quotations used elsewhere in this study there are available, of course, further examples of almost all usages shortly to be described. *Moby-Dick* and *Paradise Lost*, because of their importance, are the reservoirs from which most of the illustrations have been drawn, although for the sake of convenience some material from Milton's minor poems appears here rather than in the previous chapter, and some references occur to other works by Melville.

In the preceding section were mentioned some of Melville's paraphrases which would not strike many readers as unusual. On the other hand, some of Melville's words stud his pages conspicuously and contribute not insignificantly to the symphonic quality of his prose. Redburn, who once tried "to talk in Addisonian English," and whose father had owned "a fine library edition of the *Spectator*, in six large volumes,"[42] may have read, in Addison's important critical papers on *Paradise Lost*, a justification of poetic diction:

> It is not ... sufficient, that the Language of an Epic Poem be Perspicuous, unless it be also Sublime. To this end it ought to deviate from the common Forms and ordinary Phrases of Speech. . . . [The belief] that he might the better deviate

37

from the Language of the Vulgar . . . recommended to [Milton] . . . several old Words, which also makes his Poem appear the more venerable, and gives it a greater Air of Antiquity.[43]

For these or other reasons but with these and other results, Melville did use poetic diction, and used it rather freely. Furthermore, much of his poetic diction—occurring, to be sure, in other poets than Milton—can be found in the *Paradise Lost* which Melville quoted so often. Among the "poetic" words common to both are *bosky, emprise, finny, supernal, verdant, ycleped,* and many others.[44]

Some of Melville's readers may have been struck not only by his continuing the use of poetic archaisms, but also by his use of familiar words in unfamiliar senses. Certainly a second characteristic of Melville's diction is his use of some words in senses particularly dependent on the meanings of Latin roots.[45] Such usage is less common in Melville than in Milton, but exact parallels in their uses of certain words can be found:

They . . . warped the *devoted* boats toward the planted irons.
[Satan's] wicked tents *devoted.*[46]

Nor did it remain unwarranted by the *event.*
That strife/Was not inglorious, though the *event* was dire.[47]

As dreamy nature, feeling sure
Of all her *genial* labour done.
Fermented the great mother to conceive
Satiate with *genial* moisture.[48]

We strolled along . . . , *inspiring* the musky, midnight air.
[Satan sat] close at the ear of Eve/. . . *inspiring* venom.[49]

The ultimate chase of Moby-Dick . . . that *mortal* monster.
That forbidden tree, whose *mortal* taste.[50]

Strange is that text St. Matthew won
From gray Hosea in *sentence:* . . . .
My *sentence* is for open war.[51]

To gag in death the *vital* jaw of the whale.
Thee I revisit safe,/And feel thy sovran *vital* lamp.[52]

Here, as elsewhere, it is plausible—if indeed not probable—that Melville's somewhat unusual use of these words resulted from conscious or unconscious imitation of Milton, and that his similar use of the Latin meanings of other words[53] was stimulated by Milton's

38

practice. Melville's understanding of these Latin meanings, as well as of the Latin constructions which will soon be discussed, was made possible by his reasonably good knowledge of Latin.[54] His use of Latin words and constructions must have been encouraged by Milton's example.

The use of <u>archaisms</u> and of words in their root meanings increases a writer's vocabulary by making available to him the words of the past as well as those of whatever is for him the present. But a richer present and perhaps the future itself are available also, through slight deviations from the normal uses of familiar words. The deviations which were common to Melville and to Milton were the use of rare compounds and the use of words in unusual grammatical functions.

Both Melville and Milton were fond of <u>hyphenated</u> words. In this connection we should note Raymond Dexter Havens' conclusion that to trace the influence of *Paradise Lost* on eighteenth-century English poetry, "we have only to discover [the] outstanding characteristics which were thought to distinguish it alike from other poetry and from prose, and to search for them in later poetry." Among the nine characteristics which Havens mentions and to which we shall have cause to refer again, are "unusual compound epithets, formations probably borrowed from Homer, and much more frequent in *Comus* than in the later poems."[55] Some sense of Melville's extreme fondness for the same kind of word can be caught from his description in *Mardi* of a sphere where

> spirits sailed, like *broad-winged crimson-dyed* flamingos, spiralling in *sunset-clouds*. But a sadness glorified, *deep-fringed* their mystic temples, crowned with weeping halos, *bird-like*.[56]

As a matter of fact, neither Milton nor Melville confined himself to the use of compound epithets, but employed also compound nouns, verbs, and adverbs. Melville is probably the bolder of the two in his freak marriages, perhaps because of the prevailing American fondness for compounds;[57] nevertheless, both authors are remarkably similar in this respect. Both added adjectives to adjectives, nouns, and participles; adverbs to participles; and nouns to adjectives, nouns, and participles, bringing vigorous, fresh words into their narratives. For example, Milton's "timely-happy" is like Melville's "gloomy-jolly." In each of the following pairs Milton's member again precedes Melville's: "slow-endeavouring," "soft-cymballing"; "over-laboured," "over-arboured"; "tongue-doughty," "life-restless"; "chamber-ambushes," "cavern-pagoda"; and "coral-paven," "coral-hung." Of particular interest also is the large number of compounds with *all* which both authors used.[58]

Another trait which Havens used in identifying Milton's influence was "the use of one part of speech for another. Other poets have resorted to this practice, but none so often as Milton. . . . One interchange . . . that was a favorite with Milton and his followers is the use of an adjective where an adverb would ordinarily be employed."[59] There is, therefore, an interesting parallel between such sentences as these:

Melville:　The pure-watered diamond drop will *healthful* glow.
Milton:　His proud step he *scornful* turn'd.[60]

Melville:　　　The Jew they espy
　　　　Coasting *inquisitive* the shore
　　　　And *frequent* stooping.
Milton:　Angels to and fro/Pass'd *frequent*.[61]

But perhaps even more conspicuous in Milton[62] and Melville, and certainly more important for our present purposes, is the use of an adjective for a noun, where Melville seems clearly to have followed Milton's lead. Much more significant than their common use of *wet* as a noun[63] and of *azure* as synonymous with *clear sky*[64] are such parallels as these:

Melville:　The bottomless *profound* of the sea.
　　　　The speechless *profound* of the sea.
Milton:　I travel this *profound*.[65]

Melville:　That howling *infinite*.
Milton:　The void and formless *infinite*.[66]

Melville:　　　Nor thought can attain
　　　　To the placid *supreme* in the sweep of his reign.
Milton:　By mastering Heaven's *Supreme*.[67]

Both authors used the adjective *thwart* as a verb meaning *move across*,[68] and both occasionally used an adjective as a verb, and a verb as a noun, as in Melville's

> mightiest Mississippies of the land *swift* and swerve about,
> mute with *amaze,*

and Milton's

> to *better* us and *worse* our foes,
> *Amaze* . . . and terrour seiz'd the rebel host.[69]

A final type of interchange to be noted is the use of <u>nouns as verbs</u>. This transformation often appears in the form of a participle apparently developed from a noun-verb. Examples from Melville are to the left; from Milton, to the right:

| | |
|---|---|
| gemmed with diadems | trees . . . gemm'd/Their blossoms |
| bucaniers . . . hived their gold | fuell'd entrails |
| monsters rafting the sea | roses bushing round |
| musked mariners | his consorted Eve |
| orbed like shields[70] | his orbed shield[71] |

A third and final way in which both Milton and Melville transformed familiar words was by fresh uses of familiar prefixes and suffixes. One type of such change involves the use of *-est* to form unusual superlatives like Milton's "constantest" or "famousest," like Melville's "arrantest" or "abstractest."[72] Next is their unusual predilection for strange compounds of the prefix *un-,* such as "unhidebound" and "uninterpenetratingly."[73] Lastly,[74] both authors enjoyed unusual adjectives derived from proper nouns and ending in *-ean* or *-ian,* a "characteristic of *Paradise Lost* which might perhaps appear in any writer whether he knew the epic or not, but which is apt to give lines a Miltonic ring."[75]

In unusual compound words, in shifts in the grammatical functions of words, and in the uses of prefixes and suffixes, lie three additional ways in which both Melville and Milton added breadth and vigor to their vocabularies. In these areas as well as in those of poetic diction and Latinisms, Melville used not only many of Milton's words, but, perhaps more important, many of Milton's sources of words, his type of vocabulary. —

Yet we must not forget to apply a general question which we posed when we were about to "push off, *velis et remis.*"[76] Why did Melville use these Miltonic elements in his vocabulary? I know of no evidence which can answer that query directly. We must sur-

41

mise. Before we can surmise, however, we must remember that Melville's formal schooling was finished by his fifteenth birthday,[77] so that few pedants had opportunities to hammer his mind into a fixed and commonplace mold, to fasten upon him either Addison or Johnson as a model for authors of prose. Even more than is the case with most authors, Melville was forced to teach himself to write.

It may have been that during many hours of composition Melville set himself to imitating some of Milton's traits of style. This is unlikely, however. For one reason, although Melville borrowed other men's chapters, he never remained one man's debtor for long. Then too, conscious effort would have led to a much more slavish imitation than we are dealing with.

It seems more probable that although Melville's notice of Milton's peculiarities of style may not have resulted in sustained imitation, it may have emboldened the less experienced author to be irregular where the recognized master was so. In other words, Milton's example strengthened Melville in certain tendencies which his own needs helped to develop. And those needs sprang from a romantic and virtually undisciplined mind. Melville was a birthright romanticist; he almost flapped his wings as he exulted, "I write precisely as I please" and "for my humour's sake."[78] If he wished to write poetic prose, if he aimed for sublimity of expression with a tinge of antiquity, if he wished a style sometimes sterling and sometimes plated, if he would please his own whims or irritate the public's bourgeois expectations, no one, not even Poverty, was going to say him nay, and "Quips, and Cranks, and wanton Wiles" from many times and places, including Milton's Paradise, were going to serve the art of a nineteenth-century American.

And Melville was in haste. He wrote rapidly, under tremendous nervous and financial pressure. It was not mere facetiousness that caused him to ask Duyckinck for "about fifty fast-writing youths . . . because," as he added, "I have planned about that number of future works & cant find enough time to think about them separately."[79] By the use of such a superlative as "etherealest" or such compounds as "devious-cruising," "death-glorious," and "whale-commanders," his racing brain could unburden itself in a kind of shorthand. Each such word was like one of those "highly useful, *multum in parvo*, Sheffield contrivances."[80] Each archaism and

Latinism fed the restive energy, the bold iconoclasm of his mind. ⌣

Many of the same motives help to explain Melville's probable debt to Milton for certain peculiarities of sentence structure and word arrangement. One method by which both authors frequently wrought ordinary words into extraordinary patterns was repetition,[81] with its cousin, parallelism.[82] In its simplest form a single ⌣ word was repeated:

Melville:  *heavenly* vouchers of all our *heavenly* homes
Milton:    *erect* and tall,/Godlike *erect*.[83]

Other and more complex repetitions can be found in each author's *repetitions* works.[84] The extremes of complexity occur in these not dissimilar passages:

From throbbing neck-bands, and swinging belly-bands of gay-hearted horses, the sleigh-bells chimingly jingle;—but Pierre sits there in his room; Thanksgiving comes, with its glad thanks, and crisp turkeys;—but Pierre sits there in his room; soft through the snows, on tinted Indian moccasin, Merry Christmas comes stealing;—but Pierre sits there in his room; it is New Year's, and like a great flagon, the vast city over-brims at all curb-stones, wharves, and piers, with bubbling jubilations;—but Pierre sits there in his room:—Nor jingling sleigh-bells at throbbing neck-band, or swinging belly-band; nor glad thanks, and crisp turkeys of Thanksgiving; nor tinted Indian moccasin of Merry Christmas softly stealing through the snows; nor New Year's curb-stones, wharves, and piers, over-brimming with bubbling jubilations:—Nor jingling sleigh-bells, nor glad Thanksgiving, nor Merry Christmas, nor jubilating New Year's:—Nor Bell, Thank, Christ, Year;—none of these are for Pierre.

Sweet is the breath of Morn, her rising sweet,
With charm of earliest birds: pleasant the sun,
When first on this delightful land he spreads
His orient beams, on herb, tree, fruit, and flower,
Glistering with dew: fragrant the fertile earth
After soft showers; and sweet the coming on
Of grateful Evening mild; then silent Night,
With this her solemn bird, and this fair moon,
And these the gems of Heaven, her starry train:
But neither breath of Morn, when she ascends
With charm of earliest birds; nor rising sun
On this delightful land; nor herb, fruit, flower,
Glistering with dew; nor fragrance after showers;
Nor grateful evening mild; nor silent Night,
With this her solemn bird, nor walk by moon,
Or glittering star-light, without thee is sweet.[85]

43

Closely linked to such repetitions are two other conspicuous uses of words—puns and series. Melville may have punned because of Milton's example, though more probably because of Shakespeare's.[86] When he used a series of nouns, verbs, or adjectives, however, it seems rather clear that he wrote in the Miltonic tradition:[87]

> An amphitheatrical bay like Rio—belted about by the most varied and charming scenery of hill, dale, moss, meadow, court, castle, tower, grove, vine, vineyard, aqueduct, palace, square, island, fort.

> The church and cloisters, courts and vaults, lanes and passages, banquet-halls, refectories, libraries, terraces, gardens, broad walks, domicils, and dessert-rooms.[88]

Both of these passages bear comparison with one from *Paradise Regained:* Satan shows to Christ imperial Rome,

> With towers and temples proudly elevate
> On seven small hills, with palaces adorn'd,
> Porches, and theatres, baths, aqueducts,
> Statues, and trophies, and triumphal arcs,
> Gardens and groves.[89]

A particular aspect of such cumulations, and one which should require no illustration for any reader of Milton, is the massing together of proper nouns and of adjectives derived from them. Havens used this as one of the hallmarks of Milton's influence,[90] and even a single reading of *Paradise Lost* imprints the characteristic on minds less impressionable than Melville's. A comparable remark might well be made about *Mardi*, and the device appears elsewhere, though with less frequency, in Melville's other works.[91] Whitman amassed the common nouns of every-day life; Melville and Milton amassed the proper nouns of literary life. The purpose of the latter pair was to suggest authority, grandeur, and extent of both time and space. To help give universality to his story of Nantucket whalers, Melville enlists Perseus, St. George, Hercules, Jonah, and Vishnu as whalemen.[92] But in an earlier book he had employed the same method in a way strongly suggestive of a source in *Paradise Lost*. The earlier book is *Mardi*:

> Not greener that midmost terrace of the Andes, which under a torrid meridian steeps fair Quito in the dews of a perpetual spring;—not greener the nine

thousand feet of Pirohitee's tall peak, which, rising from out the warm bosom of Tahiti, carries all summer with it into the clouds;—nay, not greener the famed gardens of Cyprus,—than the vernal lawn, the knoll, the dale of beautiful Verdanna.[93]

The possible source in *Paradise Lost* is this:

> Not that fair field
> Of Enna, where Proserpine gathering flowers,
> Herself a fairer flower by gloomy Dis
> Was gather'd which cost Ceres all that pain
> To seek her through the world; nor that sweet grove
> Of Daphne by Orontes, and the inspir'd
> Castalian spring, might with this Paradise
> Of Eden strive; nor that Nyseian isle
> Girt with the river Triton, where old Cham,
> Whom Gentiles Ammon call and Libyan Jove,
> Hid Amalthea, and her florid son
> Young Bacchus, from his stepdame Rhea's eye;
> Nor where Abassin kings their issue guard,
> Mount Amara, though this by some suppos'd
> True Paradise under the Ethiop line
> By Nilus' head, enclos'd with shining rock,
> A whole day's journey high, but wide remote
> From this Assyrian garden.[94]

A further characteristic of both Melville's and Milton's pages is frequent use of parenthetical remarks. A German scholar, Walter Weber, has noted it as an idiosyncrasy of Melville; Havens has noted it in Milton;[95] and, to be sure, authors like Whitman have exceeded both Melville and Milton in the use of the device. Parentheses may both suggest speed and aid condensation in expression. They may, therefore, have appealed to both Melville and Milton for the reasons that compound words appealed to them. In addition, parentheses frequently serve the needs of writers whose involved thoughts can best be expressed in involved sentences. Milton and Melville were such writers. In Melville's case, the use of parentheses may have been further encouraged by his having to do much of his writing in great haste.

Havens, who mentions the value of condensation as a probable cause of Milton's fondness for parentheses, gives the same reason for the existence of another outstanding trait of his style, "the omission of words not necessary to the sense."[96] Such ellipses are much more frequent in *Paradise Lost* than in Melville's works, but a few omissions form a minute part of the answer to the question of how *Moby-Dick* came to be its own glorious self.

The prose from which such omissions have been made is, of course, set apart from more orthodox writing. It may be set apart in the direction of that sublimity which both Milton and Melville so often achieved, and to which, according to Addison as already quoted, "Old Words" make another contribution. A further method which Addison recommended for

> raising the Language, and giving it a Poetical Turn, is to make use of the Idioms of other Tongues. . . . *Milton*, in conformity with the Practice of the Ancient Poets, and with *Aristotle's* Rule has infused a great many *Latinisms* . . . into the Language of his Poem. . . . Under this Head may be reckoned the placing the Adjective after the Substantive, the transposition of Words, the turning the Adjective into a Substantive, with several other Foreign Modes of Speech, which this Poet has naturalized to give his Verse the greater Sound, and throw it out of Prose.[97]

The method of "turning the Adjective into a Substantive" has already been cited as a practice which Melville may have derived from Milton. But the two other Latinisms which Addison mentions, and which Havens also emphasizes,[98] were likewise employed by Melville in conscious or unconscious imitation of Milton.

"Placing the Adjective after the Substantive" is used by both Milton and Melville when only one adjective is involved, and also, more conspicuously, when two are used, one before and one after the noun. Readers of *Paradise Lost* should be familiar with such transpositions as "voice divine," "flying steed unrein'd," "heavenly form Angelic," and "unvoyageable gulf obscure."[99] Melville's usage occurs in such phrases as "panoply complete," "twilight glade, interminable," "interesting items contingent," and "good fare and plenty, fine flip and strong."[100] Some of these examples from both authors bear juxtaposition:

Melville: dusky tribes innumerable
Milton:   upright beams innumerable[101]

          The Blocksberg's demons dire.
          Hydras and Chimeras dire[102]

          A hooked, Roman bill sublime
          In the dun air sublime[103]

46

> of some dark hope forlorn
> in these wild woods forlorn[104]

In Melville's as in Milton's works are dozens upon dozens of these adjective-noun-adjective locutions. In *Clarel* occurs "Through twilight of mild evening pale";[105] the phrase repeats no precise series of words from Milton, but like many of Melville's phrases it does repeat a pattern of grammar which casts over numbers of Melville's pages an almost elusive aura of Miltonism.

The use of a postpositional adjective is, as Addison states, but one of several Latin transpositions of words found in Milton. Melville exhibits a like variety of transpositions.[106] In some of these a split occurs; for example, one part of a compound subject precedes the verb whereas the other part follows the verb. Numerous examples of the four following types of inversions could be found.

*Inverted subject and predicate:*

Melville: And heaved and heaved, still unrestingly heaved the black sea.
Wisdom is vain, and prophesy.
Milton: Nor stood unmindful Abdiel to annoy
The atheist crew.

Strange horror seize thee, and pangs unfelt before.[107]

*Inverted predicate adjective:*

Pretty sure am I.
Top-heavy was the ship.

Displeas'd/All were who heard.[108]

*Inverted adverbial phrase:*

Palms, alpacas, and volcanoes, . . . are *in luxuriant profusion* stamped.
But while [the carpenter was] now *upon so wide a field thus variously* accomplished. . . .

O thou, that *with surpassing glory* crown'd. . . .
She turns, *on hospitable thoughts* intent.[109]

*Inverted object and verb:*

In what time of tempest, to what seagull's scream, the crowning eddies did their work, knows no mortal man.
We sailed from sea to sea; . . . vast empires explored, and inland valleys to their utmost heads.

Whence thou return'st, and whither went'st, I know.
[Adam and Eve] Firm peace recover'd soon, and wonted calm.[110]

Two other Latin grammatical patterns which both Melville and Milton used are an imitation of the ablative absolute and suspension. The former of these is not, however, at all common in Melville.[111] The latter is, and so provides a closer link with Milton. James Holly Hanford calls suspension "an authentic character of Milton's utterance and one which contributes more perhaps than any other single element to the elevation of his poetic style."[112] Sometimes in *Paradise Lost* as many as four or five lines separate subjects from their verbs,[113] while less lengthy suspensions are very frequent. In Melville there are equal variations in the length of suspensions; but let two examples from two successive pages suffice:

> The mariner, when drawing nigh the coasts of foreign lands, if by night he hear the roar of breakers, starts to vigilance. . . .
> Tell me, why this strong young colt, foaled in some peaceful valley of Vermont, far removed from all beasts of prey—why is it that upon the sunniest day, if you but shake a fresh buffalo robe behind him, so that he cannot even see it, but only smells its wild animal muskiness—why will he start, snort, and with bursting eyes paw the ground in frenzies of affright?[114]

Of this characteristic of Melville's style Weber has remarked,

> The manifestations of syntactical suspension . . . are caused by Melville's strongly emotional form of expression. To be sure, Melville thereby places himself in the ranks of poets, at whose head Milton stands, whose wealth of suspension in syntax left behind them far-reaching after-effects in literature.[115]

This statement raises a question which undoubtedly hovers over many of the preceding and some of the following pages: Could not Melville have derived many of these characteristics from other sources than Milton? The answer is, of course, Yes. But that answer carries with it two qualifications, without which it does not represent the whole truth. In the first place, many of the authors who could have influenced Melville on these points could have done so only because they themselves had imitated Milton. Merely a glance at Havens' Table of Contents, with its chapters on Milton's influence on Pope, Thomson, Young, Cowper, Ossian, Blake, Wordsworth, Keats, Shelley, Byron, and others, should shake any skeptic on this point. What Melville did not drink at its source, he might have imbibed after it had mixed with other tributaries, or, conceivably, after it had flowed into the sea of common speech.

48

But then, in the second place, one must prove that Melville was familiar with these other potential influences[116] and establish the date of his becoming familiar with them. Carlyle is a case in point here. Similarities between his style and that of Melville in *Pierre* have been indicated by Robert S. Forsythe.[117] An influence seems possible, for we know that Melville read Carlyle in 1850, two years before *Pierre* was published.[118] However, many of the characteristics which Forsythe connects with Carlyle are shown, through the present study, to be traceable to Milton. Yet we can hardly leave the matter with the statement that Melville derived those traits from either Carlyle or Milton, for by 1850, the date of the earliest known contact between Carlyle and Melville, Melville had already demonstrated not only his familiarity with Milton's works, but also the presence in his style of the characteristics in question.

We shall later see that Melville probably knew the Bible and Shakespeare better than he knew Milton,[119] but I sincerely doubt that any sources other than those were as much a part of his mind for so long a period as were some of Milton's poems. The gates of direct influence from Milton to Melville were open; those from many other possible parallel influences were not.

# CHAPTER FOUR

# POETIC AND EPIC
# INFLUENCES OF *PARADISE LOST*

> " *The secrets of the currents in the
> seas have never yet been divulged,
> even to the most erudite research.*"
> —Moby-Dick, *I, 226.*

A⊤ times during the preceding chapter it has probably seemed
strange that prose works should be compared at such length with
poems. Actually, of course, we have been dealing chiefly with prose
marked by many of the characteristics of poetry, and with poetry
which lacks some of the most obvious and superficial aspects of
verse, such as rhyme and emphasis on the line as a unit. Nor could
this study be by any means the first to call Melville an author of
poetic prose, or <u>Moby-Dick</u> an epic. In fact, Melville himself was
the first to link his <u>masterpiece with poetry</u>.

> The "whaling voyage" . . . will be a strange sort of a book, tho', I fear; blubber is
> blubber you know; tho' you may get oil out of it, the poetry runs as hard as sap
> from a frozen maple tree.[1]

And in the finished book itself he wrote, significantly,

> Now it remains to conclude the last chapter of this part of the description
> by rehearsing—*singing*, if I may—the romantic proceeding of decanting off
> [leviathan's] oil.[2]

In our own century, John Erskine has made the statement about
Ahab's tale that

> when we say that this story is a poem rather than a novel, we mean that its art
> consists not in reproducing pictures of the outside of life, such as we can call

50

faithful, but rather in preparing our minds for an effect of emotion, so that at the end there will be a powerful catharsis, or release of feeling. . . .

Though written in prose it has the power of a great epic—that is, it gathers up our emotions around a central figure, a central incident, and one central mood.[3]

Sealts, Mumford, Forsythe, and F. B. Freeman[4] too have used *epic* in connection with *Moby-Dick,* and Padraic Colum enlarges on the same theme by defining the book as an epic

in the sense of compositions that have a far-reaching theme, a high and singular style, a multiplicity of interest, a tragic and heroic outlook. . . . If Melville had consciously proposed to himself to make an epic of man's invasion of the oceans, his theme and his handling of it could hardly, it seems to me, be different.[5]

Certainly *Moby-Dick* fits Erskine's definition of poetry and Colum's definition of epic, but what about other definitions? To what degree do these authors use the words *poem* or *epic* in a very loose fashion, and to what degree are they prepared for close examination? Students of the dramatic structure of *Paradise Lost* and of *Moby-Dick* have, independently of one another, published conclusions which merit some comparison,[6] but there seem to have been no sustained attempts to analyze the influence of the epic type on Melville's work. The whole of such an analysis lies beyond the proper scope of this book, but it is necessary to enumerate some qualities of poetry and of epic held in common by Milton's poem and Melville's novel. In doing so one might demonstrate the remarkable extent to which the statements just quoted about *Moby-Dick* apply to *Paradise Lost* and, vice versa, how true of *Moby-Dick* are statements like this by Addison, made in a criticism of Milton:

Besides the hidden Meaning of an Epic Allegory, the plain literal Sense ought to appear probable. The story should be such as an ordinary Reader may Acquiesce in, whatever Natural Moral or Political Truth may be discovered in it by Men of greater Penetration.[7]

In lieu of such demonstrations, this chapter will emphasize certain specific similarities in technique which again indicate at least a Miltonic flavor, and perhaps a Miltonic influence. The roles of the heroes, Satan and Ahab, however, must be considered in a later section.

Alliteration is one of Melville's most frequently used borrowings from the poets. Sometimes, as in the first of the following quotations, he uses it to link merely a pair of words; sometimes, as in the second, he unites a number of words, now with inartistic bluntness, again with merriment. On still other occasions, however, alliteration furthers the more serious ambitions of his art, as it did with Milton.

> *H*overingly *h*alting, and dipping on the wing, the white sea-fowls *l*ongingly *l*ingered over the agitated pool that he left.

> What *b*itter *b*lanks in those *b*lack-*b*ordered marbles which cover no ashes.

> It was while gliding through these latter waters that one serene and moonlight night, when all the waves rolled by like scrolls of silver; and, by their soft, suffusing seethings, made what seemed a silvery silence, not a solitude: on such a silent night a silvery jet was seen far in advance of the white bubbles at the bow.[8]

Obviously no use of italics could adequately point out the lovely interfusions in this "liquid sea of sound."[9] Of all the poets who might have influenced Melville towards such unusual sound-painting in prose,

> undoubtedly the pre-eminent influence is that of Milton, who through his wonderfully perfected, musical, and yet so weighty language, held Melville in his thrall all his life. Like Melville, Milton also had an extremely delicate ear for consonance and sound values.[10]

One device which adds immeasurably to the beauty of the long, suspended sentence last quoted from Melville is its fundamentally iambic rhythm. Melville's lapses or risings into such a beat have been frequently commented on,[11] and parts of *Moby-Dick* have been printed as more than passable blank verse.[12] One passage which I believe has not previously been printed in its natural pentameter lines is about the *Pequod's* blacksmith:

> Harkening to these voices, East and West,
> By early sunrise, and by fall of eve,
> The blacksmith's soul responded, Ay, I come!
> And so Perth went a-whaling.[13]

Just as in "The Paradise of Bachelors" Melville used the rhythm of "Il Penseroso," so here in *Moby-Dick* he used that of Milton's epics, achieving something far subtler than just an iambic pentameter rhythm—a Miltonic ring. Weber says that

> Melville's tendency is in general towards a fundamentally iambic prose rhythm as it found its ideal form in Miltonic heroic verse and in dramatic blank verse.[14]

It is true, of course, that much of Melville's rhythmic prose has a Shakespearean tone to it,[15] but in weighing Shakespeare's influence against Milton's it is important to remember that Melville did not become intimately acquainted with Shakespeare until after he had written his first iambic prose, and after he had read Milton with some attention. It was on February 24, 1849, that Melville wrote to Duyckinck,

> Dolt & ass that I am I have lived more than 29 years, & until a few days ago, never made close acquaintance with the divine William. . . . I am mad to think how minute a cause has prevented me hitherto from reading Shakespeare.[16]

One month before that statement Melville had signed the preface to *Mardi*,[17] and the book appeared for sale in London only twenty days after the letter was written.[18] Consequently it was well before his intimacy with Shakespeare that Melville wrote this blank verse in prose:

> As when from howling Rhœtian heights,  ◡ | ◡ |
> The traveller spies green Lombardy below,
> And downward rushes toward that pleasant plain;
> So, sloping from long rolling swells,
> At last we launched upon the calm lagoon.[19]

But in this liquid passage we have not only rhythm, alliteration, and an indefinable timbre, which are reminiscent of Milton; we have also an epic simile.

> If we look into the Conduct of *Homer*, *Virgil* and *Milton*, as the great Fable is the Soul of each Poem, so to give their Works an agreeable Variety, their Episodes are so many short Fables, and their Similes so many short Episodes.[20]

Thus wrote Addison. Melville continued this epic tradition throughout *Moby-Dick*. Sometimes he put his epic similes into iambic pentameter patterns. When this is so, his rhythmic prose is most markedly Miltonic, just as his most Shakespearean tones occur in dramatic speeches. In the separate forms of simile and dialogue, Melville's fabric bears the stamp of the finest master in English of each form:

> As the unsetting Polar star,
> Which through the live-long, Artic, six months' night
> Sustains its piercing, steady, central gaze;
> So Ahab's purpose now fixedly gleamed down
> Upon the constant midnight of the gloomy crew.[21]

As with Milton's, Melville's epic similes are occasionally elaborated at greater length, and sometimes they are grouped close to one another,[22] as with these examples from the same paragraph:

> As a pilot, when about losing sight of a coast, whose general trending he well knows, and which he desires shortly to return to again, but at some further point; like as this pilot stands by his compass, and takes the precise bearing of the cape at present visible, in order the more certainly to hit aright the remote, unseen headland, eventually to be visited: so does the fisherman, at his compass, with the whale. . . . And as the mighty iron leviathan of the modern railway is so familiarly known in its every pace, that, with watches in their hands, men time his rate as doctors that of a baby's pulse; and lightly say of it, the up train or the down train will reach such or such a spot, at such or such an hour; even so, almost, there are occasions when these Nantucketers time that other leviathan of the deep.[23]

Like these last, some of Milton's similes had been drawn from everyday life,[24] and like others of Milton's, some of Melville's were drawn from travel, history, and other learned or unusual sources.[25]

One critic who has briefly analyzed Melville's use of Homeric similes to add bulk and stature to the White Whale and his pursuer, has continued,

> He had made one or two flat attempts to handle . . . [similes] in *Mardi*; and his general interest in Homer was to be shown several years later by his frequent markings in Arnold's essay on how to translate him, and by his enthusiasm for Chapman's version. But what Melville had learned in *Moby-Dick* that he had not known in *Mardi* came not from Homer, but from his own assimilation of the organic principle. He had learned how to make beauty . . . functional, for, unlike most borrowers, he did not let his Homeric similes remain mere ornaments.

The flatness of the similes in *Mardi* is certainly open to question. And surely in addition to Melville's "own assimilation of the organic principle," or as an aid to it, one should mention the example of Milton. Milton was not the artist to use Homeric similes for "mere ornaments," and Melville must have learned much of Homer's art through Homer's presence in *Paradise Lost*.

The critic continues,

54

> There could hardly be a more integral way of giving body to Ahab's _hubris_ than by the image of the towering elm about to call down heaven's thunderbolt.[26]

The reference is to another iambic passage:

> As in the hurricane that sweeps the plain,
> Men fly the neighborhood of some lone,
> Gigantic elm, whose very height and strength
> But render it so much the more unsafe,
> Because so much the more a mark for thunderbolts;
> So at those last words of Ahab's
> Many of the mariners did run
> From him in a terror of dismay.[27]

Such a figure is most justly praised for its functionalism, but there is no very great step to this simile from the following one in _Paradise Lost:_

> Millions of Spirits for his fault amerc'd
> Of Heaven, and from eternal splendours flung
> For his revolt; yet faithful . . . stood,
> Their glory wither'd: as when Heaven's fire
> Hath scath'd the forest oaks, or mountain pines,
> With singed top their stately growth, though bare,
> Stands on the blasted heath.[28]

There is one other device for which Melville has been given credit which he should share with Milton and others. A claim that the interior monologue appeared first in modern literature in 1886 has been refuted by pointing out that

> three complete chapters in [_Moby-Dick_] . . . and many other passages, are but lengthy soliloquies which, in modern parlance, we should call interior monologues, since they are not spoken but represent the thought processes of . . . characters.[29]

As has already been indicated, some of Melville's soliloquies appear to find their prototypes in Shakespeare's. Yet there is a slight step from dramatic monologue to fictional thought. Consequently, in this respect Shakespeare is not so immediate a source as is Milton, who had already taken that step, using, in his own extended narrative, soliloquies precisely like Melville's.[30] Satan, Adam, and Eve are in all such cases said to have spoken, though that they spoke merely in silence to themselves can be presumed on the basis of this line preceding Adam's first reaction to Eve's trespass:

55

First to himself he inward silence broke.[31]

In such monologues as well as in other speeches of their characters, as also in passages of exposition, both Milton and Melville show a further similarity—frequent bursts of emotion expressed in passages of pathos. Milton himself breaks out,

> O! when meet now
> Such pairs, in love and mutual honour join'd?

or

> How didst thou grieve then, Adam!

or he has Eve apostrophize,

> O flowers
> That never will in other climate grow![32]

Melville was apparently equally surcharged with emotion, which his romanticism vented in such exclamations as

> Oh! ye whose dead lie buried beneath the green grass!
> Oh, Ahab! what shall be grand in thee, it must needs be plucked at from the skies.

Or a character calls,

> Oh! thou clear spirit of clear fire, whom on these seas I as Persian once did worship.[33]

Weber says of this aspect of Melville's style,

> That which we meet in the rest of literature let us say as emphasis, must be considered as more or less formal rhetorical technique. That is in large measure the case with Milton. To be sure it is just his lofty pathos which leads directly over to the subjective outbreak of feeling typical of romanticism. Therefore we sense behind many pathetic passages in Melville's works the great example of Milton.[34]

In addition to the alliteration, rhythm, similes, soliloquies, and pathos which *Paradise Lost* and *Moby-Dick* have in common[35]—superimposed on similarities of vocabulary and sentence structure—there are some miscellaneous likenesses in techniques or structure. Melville's tale, for instance, begins in the middle of Ahab's feud with the White Whale, as Milton's begins in the middle of Satan's story; and both stories are marked by physical conflict and by traditional epic taunts and boastings. Furthermore, in both narratives the initially predominant character loses importance as

56

another major figure, the author's intended hero, gains the stage: Ishmael fades as Ahab brightens, and Satan fades before Mankind. In both works the endings are revealed early by hints and statements of the outcome,[36] but the actual working out of the conclusions is delayed by digressions and interpolations, which strict classicists might wish expunged from each.[37] Melville digresses on whaling and Milton on theology and cosmology, while both halt to talk about themselves and are happy in their mixtures of science with pseudo-science. "The Town-Ho's Story" is a narrative within a narrative, as are Raphael's and Michael's longest speeches, with the same interruptions of the inner narratives to remind us of their dependence on the main story. The flow from the personal to the central to the peripheral and back again is very free. But in all cases, the apparent delays of the central action are necessary to the creation, in characters and readers, of understandings or attitudes vital to proper reactions when the climaxes arise.

Yet none of these matters, true parallels though they are, are essential to an epic.[38] An epic is to be identified not by similes or metaphors or a descent into hell, but by other less superficial characteristics. Those less superficial characteristics we are now in a position to discuss. In considering them we must focus our attention more sharply than ever on *Moby-Dick*, to the exclusion of Melville's other works, and we shall judge *Moby-Dick* not by what critics of Melville think an epic should be, but by what Lascelles Abercrombie, a critic of the epic, thinks an epic is. Nor will it seem necessary to point out in detail that *Paradise Lost* is an epic, and that, as the epic which Melville probably knew better than any other, it may well have influenced him in making *Moby-Dick* the generously epic book that it is.

One of the basic requirements for an epic is a story—but not any story whatsoever. The story of a true epic cannot be that of a *Rape of the Lock*, or, to come closer to home, of a *Mardi* or of a *Pierre*. The story of a true epic must not merely have "an unmistakable air of actuality"; it must be "something which indisputably, and admittedly, *has been* a human experience," whether it tells of "legendary heroism . . . or [of] actual history, as in Lucan and Camoens and Tasso."[39] Does *Moby-Dick* meet these qualifications? Certainly Melville's descriptions of whales and of the whaling in-

57

dustry have "an unmistakable air of actuality" established by his skill as an author but based on his experiences as a whale-hunter and on his wide reading in the literature of whaling. It is equally certain that the chief events of *Moby-Dick* were closely modeled upon happenings "which indisputably and admittedly" have been human experiences. During the first half of the nineteenth century, accounts of scores of whaling, trading, exploring, and missionary voyages were published, and through them ran tales of unusually vicious whales, of captains who long hunted a particular whale, and of ships sunk by whales.[40] Furthermore, the whaling industry was a major part of American economic life, and as such it influenced man's actions and thoughts to an extent best suggested by stating that it held much the same relationship to the 1830's, 40's, and 50's that aviation has held to the 1920's, 30's, and 40's.[41] Perhaps we cannot maintain that Melville's book is an epic to the extent that it uses "some great story which has been absorbed into the prevailing consciousness" of its author's country,[42] but certainly the physical environment in which his characters move was an actual one, familiar through experience or report to many of Melville's countrymen. And, by way of parenthesis, the sense of geographical scope in *Moby-Dick* is fully as great as that in *Paradise Lost*. They are both "large" stories as well as long ones.

But of course an epic is not merely a book telling a story which has an air of actuality and a background of authenticity. That story must be well and greatly told.[43] Whether *Moby-Dick* is a story well told might be determined by its popularity among adolescents as a tale of adventure. Whether it is greatly told might be determined by its popularity with adults. Or we might agree that by good and great telling we mean that the author of an epic must turn a mass of confused splendors into a grand design, forcing the parts "to obey a single presiding unity of artistic purpose." Such unity is not, of course, merely an external affair. The only thing "which can master the perplexed stuff of epic material into unity . . . is, an ability to see in particular human experience some significant symbolism of man's general destiny." The epic poet must, therefore, not merely accept the generally held facts of his era, but he must transfigure them so that they will symbolize not life itself, but some manner of life. That manner of life, based

58

on courage, should reflect the accepted unconscious metaphysic of the author's age.[44]

It seems no more necessary to prove at this point that *Moby-Dick* has a significance beyond that of the loss of a ship than to prove that *Paradise Lost* tells of more than a battle in Heaven and the eating of an apple. Indeed, the very wealth of affirmations as to just what *Moby-Dick* and *Paradise Lost* do symbolize proves that they symbolize something or nothing, and the latter alternative few will accept. It is relevant, however, to note that John Freeman, Melville's English biographer, has found *Moby-Dick* and *Paradise Lost* to have the same larger significance:

> "That intangible malignity which has been from the beginning . . . all the subtle demonisms of life and thought"—it is this and these that haunt Ahab's heart as they haunt Melville. . . .
>
> > Of man's first disobedience and the fruit
> > Of that forbidden tree whose mortal taste
> > Brought death into the world and all our woe
> > With loss of Eden—
>
> this is Melville's theme as it was Milton's, but the name of the great enemy is not Lucifer, but Leviathan. The never-to-be-ended combat typified by Milton's Lucifer and Archangels is typified as boldly by Melville's Moby-Dick and Captain Ahab. Vindicating his pride against almightiness, Lucifer is overthrown but unsubdued; but vindicating his perverted spirit against a malignity not less perverse, Ahab is slain by the White Whale.[45]

With equal profit we can come at the same conclusion from another opinion. Abercrombie writes that in *Paradise Lost* "the spirit of man is equally conscious of its own limited reality and of the unlimited reality of that which contains him and drives him with its motion—of his own will striving in the midst of destiny: destiny irresistible, yet his will unmastered."[46] God is Milton's symbol for the unlimited reality which contains man. Is not the White Whale a symbol for the same concept? Milton, true to his age, thought of irresistible destiny in terms of a divine power centered in God. Melville, equally true to his age, thought of irresistible destiny in terms of the mysterious powers of unleashed nature, best symbolized by the most powerful animate creation of nature. God was still the consciously or outwardly worshipped power of 1851, but the unconscious metaphysic of Melville's age—the age of land and sea frontiers, of growing materialism, of the exploitation of nature, and of the pre-Darwinian cuts at revelation —that metaphysic held nature as its deity to worship and to fear.

Such a manner of life—or indeed any manner of life—is best portrayed in literature through people who live, through convincing characters. It is, therefore, a further requirement of an epic that it contain at least one figure "in whom the whole virtue, and perhaps also the whole failure, of living seems superhumanly concentrated." Through that figure will be symbolized much of the meaning of the epic, and he will be its hero.

Three chapters earlier, during a discussion of the inner affinity which existed between Melville and Milton, mention was made of Melville's sharing Milton's repugnance to the traditional trappings of the military hero. From that discussion, however, should not have been inferred the notion that Melville's and Milton's characters are not heroic. Although they may lack the outward marks of Homer's heroes, they have much of their spirit: their courage and their individuality. Especially is this true of the Satan of the first six books of *Paradise Lost*, and of Ahab. They illustrate remarkably well what Abercrombie says of the morals of an heroic age:

> In Homer, for instance, it can be seen pretty clearly that a "good" man is simply a man of imposing, active individuality; . . . he who rules is thereby proven the "best." And from its nature it must be an age very heartily engaged in something; usually in fighting whoever is near enough to be fought with.

And was not a large part of the America of the nineteenth century experiencing an heroic age? Were not the Calhouns, the Thoreaus, the Astors manifesting in their very different ways that theirs was a time for "vehement private individuality freely and greatly asserting itself," even though "the assertion is not always what we should call noble"? It is relevant to note that the heroic age does not, as a rule, last very long, and that it is succeeded by "a comparatively rigid and perhaps comparatively lustreless civilization"?[47] Some of these questions can be answered only with greater perspective than we now have. Certainly the answers to them are not intended to lead to the conclusion that the century of Andrew Jackson and James Fiske was identical in spirit with the century of Achilles and Odysseus. Nevertheless, it may be valuable to think of Ahab as the hero of an epic. To do so may cast new light on the hero, on the epic, and on what the author of the epic may have learned from previous epics. A man can be a hero of primitive courage using either a sword or a prayer to God or an injunction, and fighting for either brute or spiritual or financial dominance.

To notice similarities leads, however, only half the way to wisdom's house. The rest of the way is reached by recognizing the significance of dissimilarities. There is much significance in the differences between Adam and Achilles. There is perhaps equal significance in the differences between both of them and Ahab, and between earlier epics and *Moby-Dick*. For example, that Adam in Paradise is in command of one of God's works, whereas Ahab in the Pacific is in command of a capitalistic business enterprise is not unrelated to certain theological and economic differences between Milton and Melville as individuals, and between the ages in which they lived. Meanings for other differences have already appeared in this study, and more will appear before the end.

There remains the necessity for this chapter to consider the fact that an epic poet, dealing with a story and a significance, should set them out in as lofty poetry as he can achieve.[48] Certainly Milton created *Paradise Lost* with lofty poetry. Did Melville so create *Moby-Dick*?

Much of *Moby-Dick* cannot by any sane standards be called poetry. It may be very competent prose, but it is not poetry. Yet for being prose it should, probably, be praised, not condemned, since its matter is matter best treated in prose. And perhaps it is entirely appropriate that large parts of a modern epic should be written in prose. Perhaps continuous verse is to be required of only those epics written in an age when verse is the dominant form of literary expression. In an age when prose is dominant, perhaps we should expect prose epics. Yet however this may be, some passages of *Moby-Dick* are written in a style so unlike that of most of the book that it seems to deserve a special name. "Verse" is not appropriate, but "prose-poetry" or "poetry" suggest themselves. Certainly the matter of these passages is much like the matter from which Milton and others have created unquestioned poetry. Certainly the manner of these passages has the elevation, even the ritualism, of *Paradise Lost*. And in these passages appear many of the characteristics of vocabulary, of sentence structure, and of alliteration, rhythm, similes, soliloquies, and pathos which we have termed Miltonic.

61

As has been mentioned from time to time, numerous of these characteristics are ones which Raymond Dexter Havens used as criteria of Milton's influence on English poetry. What, we may ask, is the final tally? Three characteristics of *Paradise Lost* Havens considered valueless in determining Milton's influence on authors who had read pre-Miltonic poetry, but valuable in determining why poetry sounded Miltonic. These three are repetitions of words or phrases, cumulations of the same parts of speech, and the use of adjectives ending in *-ean* or *-ian* and derived from proper nouns. All of these we have found in *Moby-Dick* and others of Melville's works. Of the nine characteristics more peculiar to Milton's epic, seven are these: inversions of natural word order, omissions of words not needed to convey the meaning, parentheses and apposition, the use of one part of speech as another, a vocabulary marked by archaisms and borrowings, generous use of proper nouns, and unusual compound epithets. Every one of these also marks Melville's style to a greater or less degree. The two traits which I have not listed are "dignity, reserve, and stateliness"; and "the organ tone, the sonorous orotund."[49] These two are also found in Melville. Moreover, the two following quotations illustrate not only the dignity and sonorousness to complete Havens' tally, but also support the contention that like other epic writers Melville set out his story and its significance in lofty poetry:

> Where unrecorded names and navies rust, and untold hopes and anchors rot; where in her murderous hold this frigate earth is ballasted with bones of millions of the drowned; there, in that awful water-land, there was thy most familiar home.

> I turn my body from the sun. What ho, Tashtego! let me hear thy hammer. Oh! ye three unsurrendered spires of mine; thou uncracked keel; and only god-bullied hull; thou firm deck, and haughty helm, Pole-pointed prow,—death-glorious ship! must ye then perish, and without me? Am I cut off from the last fond pride of meanest shipwrecked captains? Oh, lonely death on lonely life! Oh, now I feel my topmost greatness lies in my topmost grief. Ho, ho! from all your furthest bounds, pour ye now in, ye bold billows of my whole foregone life, and top this one piled comber of my death! Toward thee I roll, thou all-destroying but unconquering whale; to the last I grapple with thee.[50]

The present study has, of course, emphasized links between Milton and Melville which fell outside the purpose of Havens' analysis. Iambic rhythm, epic similes, suspensions, compounds of *all* and *un-*, and general epic characteristics are perhaps the most important of these, but the sum of them must be totaled if one is to grasp the full significance of A. S. W. Rosenbach's statement that Melville "could write with . . . the grandeur of Milton."[51] To repeat, this study does not have to do with a case of conscious imitation, nor with an unconscious, unadulterated assimilation. To some indeterminable extent it does deal with the fact that "the books . . . [which] really spoke to Melville became an immediate part of him to a degree hardly matched by any other of our great writers in their maturity."[52] It also deals with that close, attentive reading, whereby "one great Genius often catches the Flame from another, and writes in his Spirit, without copying servilely after him."[53]

Finally, let us, after all, use a method mentioned many pages earlier. In reading the first quotation, let us think how true of Melville's style is this description originally made of Milton's; and, in reading the second, let us think how true of *Paradise Lost* is the already familiar sentence concerning *Moby-Dick:*

> [Melville's] style, despite his employment of a verse form identical with the Elizabethan dramatists, stands at an opposite pole from that of Shakespeare and his colleagues. [Melville's] . . . language, unlike theirs, has little relish of the speech of men. Where their anomalies are colloquial and idiomatic, his are the product of a preference for the unusual and recondite, in vocabulary and construction, which leads him to archaism on the one hand, and to the substitution of foreign idiom, particularly Latin, for native on the other. Sometimes not even classical or earlier English example can be alleged. [Melville] . . . is simply carving for himself, remoulding and creating with fine disregard for precedent. In general, [Melville's] . . . style may be described as almost uniquely literary and intellectual. Freighted with learning and bookish phrase, elaborate in construction, often alien in vocabulary, it achieves a uniform effect of dignity and aloofness and becomes a perfect medium for the restrained and elevated yet intensely passionate personality of its author.[54]

> [*Paradise Lost*] is a symphony; every resource of language and thought, fantasy, description, philosophy, natural history, drama, broken rhythms, blank verse, imagery, symbol, are utilized to sustain and expand the great theme.

As Addison wrote in an essay on Milton,

> The Learned Reader cannot but be pleased with the Poet's Imitation of Homer.[55]

The sequence of imitation and the pleasure of learned readers were both augmented by Melville's echoing of Milton.

# CHAPTER FIVE

# PERSONS AND PLACES

*"All the world over, facts are
more eloquent than words."*
—Omoo, *p. 223.*

ALTHOUGH the present chapter is intended as a survey of Melville's use of some of the persons and places of *Paradise Lost*, its material can be exemplified by his use of only a brief, incidental image in Milton's poem:

> Oft, though wisdom wake, *suspicion* sleeps
> At wisdom's gate, and to simplicity
> Resigns her charge, while goodness thinks no ill
> Where no ill seems.[1]

The passage which appears to have grown out of these lines may at first seem to have nothing in common with them but the single word *suspicion:*

> Philosophy, knowledge, experience—were those trusty knights of the castle recreant? No, but unbeknown to them, the enemy stole on the castle's south side, its genial one, where *Suspicion*, the warder, parleyed.[2]

Yet it takes no very great imagination to realize that "wisdom's gate" in Milton is close architectural kin to Melville's "castle" of "philosophy, knowledge, experience"; that "philosophy, knowledge, experience" as well as "wisdom" were regrettably betrayed; and that in both cases the betrayer was "suspicion," in one case asleep, and in the other case, parleying "on the castle's south side, its genial one." In other words, it seems not unlikely that a description vaguely remembered from *Paradise Lost* was enough to set Melville's fancy turning in a parallel course.

Whenever a description by Milton did have this effect, it helped Melville to cope with the inability of language to accomplish the purposes of description. He recognized this inability as early as 1846, when, in describing some groves in *Typee*, he wrote, "I wish that it were possible to sketch in words this spot as vividly as I recollect it."[3] In "The Encantadas," when he was again faced with a difficult description, Melville noted a hypothetical source of the name "Encantadas," adding, "Nothing can better *suggest* the aspect of once living things malignly crumbled from ruddiness into ashes."[4] Here, in a passage to which we must soon return, Melville points to an important technique of description, and one he often used—suggestion. By using details from the backdrop of *Paradise Lost*, Melville could suggest to his readers some of the scenery created by Milton's God.

Melville did carry in his mind the scenery against which Milton's epic is acted, as we know from incontrovertible evidence. In *Redburn*, for instance, the "west front" of Carlo's hand-organ, "like the gates of Milton's heaven, . . . turns on golden hinges."[5] In Melville's next book, *White Jacket*,

> high, towering in their own turbaned snows, the far inland pinnacles [of Staten Island] loomed up, like the border of some other world. Flaming *walls* and *crystal battlements*, like the *diamond* watch-*towers* along *heaven's* furthest frontier.[6]

Several years later, in "The Encantadas," Melville surmised that

> much thus, one fancies, looks the universe from Milton's celestial *battlements*. A *boundless watery* Kentucky.[7]

Part of what Melville had in mind here was Mulciber's being thrown "Sheer o'er the *crystal battlements*." But he also remembered Satan's seat in heaven "with pyramids and *towers*/ From *diamond* quarries hewn," and Satan's distant sight of

> the empyreal Heaven, extended wide . . .
> With opal *towers* and *battlements* adorn'd.

There was also the region from which Satan had obtained that sight, part of the "*boundless* deep" and "*watery* calm" of Chaos.[8]

Chaos is, of course, a term by no means confined to Milton's works, and Melville several times used it in a way which reflects no distinguishable literary influence.[9] In one instance, however, he seems to have had in mind Milton's "several *clans*" of atoms and the attendants of Chaos' court,[10] for he wrote that

> [the sun's] light
> In time's first dawn compelled the flight
> Of Chaos' startled *clan*.[11]

Across Chaos, Sin and Death built the

> passage broad,
> Smooth, easy, inoffensive, down to Hell,[12]

which Melville remembered in Rome, when he

> started for Appian Way. Narrow,—not like Milton's Way—not suitable to dignity &c.

A later experience in Italy reminded Melville of the surroundings of Pandemonium as they may have been:

> The heigth [*sic*] & distance of these forts, their outlying loneliness. The bleakness, the savageness of glens between, seem to make Genoa rather the capital and fortified camp of Satan: fortified against the Archangels. Clouds rolling round ramparts aerial.[13]

But the scene in Milton's Hell which Melville used most frequently was the vivid one in which Satan and his followers are deceived by a grove

> laden with fair fruit, like that
> Which grew in Paradise, the bait of Eve.
> . . . Greedily they pluck'd
> The fruitage fair to sight, like that which grew
> Near that bituminous lake where Sodom flam'd;
> This more delusive, not the touch, but taste
> Deceiv'd; they, fondly thinking to allay
> Their appetite with gust, instead of fruit
> Chew'd bitter ashes, which the offended taste
> With spattering noise rejected.[14]

The apples of Sodom are not mentioned in the Bible, and many accounts mention merely their turning to ashes when touched.[15] From his recollection of Milton, Melville seems to have linked their imagined taste to their other features. During the descent into Typee, for example, he came to a stream.

> What a delicious sensation was I now to experience! I paused . . . and then im-

merged my lips in the clear element before me. Had the apples of Sodom turned to ashes in my mouth, I could not have felt a more startling revulsion.[16]

In *Moby-Dick* we are told at one point that "Ahab's glance was averted; like a blighted fruit-tree he shook, and cast his last, *cindered* apple to the soil."[17] In *The Confidence-Man* Melville used the same tradition to etch bitterness into even slight details of the background, describing an ash tray as made

in guise of an apple flushed with red and gold to the life; and, through a cleft at top, you saw it was hollow. This was for the ashes.[18]

Milton's apples also were "red and gold"—or, more exactly, "ruddy and gold."[19] The latter phrasing Melville used in *Clarel* when the travelers notice

> shrivelled nut or apple small.
> The Jew plucked one. Like a fuzz-ball
> It brake, discharging fetid dust.
> "Pippins of Sodom? they've declined!"
> Cried Derwent: "where's the *ruddy* rind?"[20]

Such apples Melville had himself seen during his visit to Palestine, and he had mentioned them in his journal, though without any Miltonic phrasing.[21]

A year or so earlier than that visit, however, this most frequently used detail from Milton's treatment of Hell had appeared in "The Encantadas." There it is part of the description in which Melville is most continuously indebted to *Paradise Lost*. The first sketch of "The Encantadas" is a general introduction stressing the desolate and forbidding nature of the group of islands. In emphasizing the "spell-bound desertness" of the isles, Melville mentioned the apples in a setting quoted in part at the beginning of this chapter:

Nothing can better suggest that aspect of once living things malignly crumbled from *ruddiness* into *ashes*. Apples of Sodom, after touching, seem these isles.

Preceding this are other phrases reminiscent of *Paradise Lost*. On the Gallipagos "no voice, no low, no howl is heard; the chief sound of life here is a hiss,"[22] just as, at the time when they tasted their deceitful fruit, Satan and his followers were plagued by "long and ceaseless hiss."[23] "Vitrified masses . . . present a most *Plutonian* sight," Melville adds on the same page, and continued, "In no world but a *fallen* one could such land exist." In the next sentence he itemizes debris which had been washed "all the way from *Paradise* to *Tartarus*."[24] Apples of Sodom, hisses, Plutonian sights, a fallen world, Paradise, and Tartarus combine to make the Encantadas hellish enough to one who can recall Milton.

Helpful as Melville may have found it to supplement his own statements with references and allusions suggesting Milton's descriptions of places, he found it even more helpful to make a similar use of Milton's descriptions of characters. God and Christ, however, are almost complete exceptions, and are such because the American could not accept the God and the Christ of *Paradise Lost* in his intellect,[25] and because in his art they are too blended with common religious concepts to provide much significant material for a study of influence. Nevertheless, a young and not fully embittered Melville sent booksellers these speculations about his "father the Deity":

> If time was, when this round *Earth* . . . was not extant; then, time may have been, when the whole material universe lived its Dark Ages; yea, when the Ineffable Silence, proceeding from its unimaginable remoteness, espied it as an isle in the sea. . . . Were all *space* a *vacuum*, yet would it be a *ful*ness; for to Himself His own universe is He.[26]

Very close to this in thought as well as wording is God's mandate to the Son before the work of creation began:

> Ride forth, and bid the Deep
> Within appointed bounds be Heaven and *Earth*;
> Boundless the Deep, because I Am who *fill*
> Infinitude, nor *vacuous* the *space*.[27]

Melville could also write Miltonically that "with Oro [God], the sun is co-eternal," but in the rest of his sentence part company with Milton by writing, "and the same life that moves that moose, animates alike the sun and Oro. All are parts of One."[28]

Much more to Melville's purposes were Milton's descriptions of the couple whom Melville dubbed "the two orchard thieves."[29] For example, two passages in *Paradise Lost* told Melville of Adam and Eve's dining at noon,[30] and were used by him to add specific detail to some waggery in *White Jacket*:

After all, though "Paradise Lost" be a noble poem, and we man-of-war's men, no doubt, largely partake in the immortality of the immortals; yet, let us candidly confess it, shipmates, that, upon the whole, our dinners are the most momentous affairs of these lives we lead beneath the moon. . . . Doubtless Adam and Eve dined at twelve.[31]

In the case of Adam's appearance, it seems probable that this description by Milton influenced the succeeding one by Melville:

> Two of far nobler shape, erect and tall,
> *God*like erect, with native honour clad
> In naked *majesty* seem'd lords of all: . . .
> His fair large front and eye sublime declar'd
> Absolute rule.[32]

A most imperial and archangelical apparition of that unfallen Western world, which . . . revived the glories of those primeval times when Adam walked *majestic* as a *god*, bluff-bowed and fearless.[33]

More evident, and twice as frequent, were Melville's borrowings from the poet's descriptions of Eve.[34] In one Book Milton had said that

> Likest . . . [*Eve*] seemed . . .
> to Ceres in her prime,
> Yet virgin of Proserpina from Jove.

By a repeated reference to Proserpina and Ceres, this passage is linked to the claim that

> not that fair field
> Of *Enna*, where *Proserpine* gathering flowers,
> Herself a fairer flower by gloomy Dis
> Was gather'd, which cost Ceres all that pain
> . . . might with this Paradise
> Of *Eden* strive.[35]

Very probably it was the ties in these lines which caused Melville to choose as he did the proper nouns for his comparison of "sweet forms of maidens" to

> *Eves* in *Edens* ere the Fall, or *Proserpines* in *Ennas*.[36]

Melville's second use of Milton's Eve occurs in a posthumous poem in which he writes to the queen of flowers, the rose,

> Scarce you would poor Adam upbraid . . .
> That the Angel indignant, with eyes that foreran

> The betrayed generations,
> Cast out the *flowers* wherewith Eve
> Decked her *nuptials* with man.[37]

This is almost certainly a reworking of a scene which Milton's superior poetry had impressed on Melville's mind. Eve has overheard the doom pronounced by Michael, the "Angel indignant," whose eyes, in Books XI and XII of *Paradise Lost*, forerun "the betrayed generations." Eve exclaims:

> O *flowers*
> That never will in other climate grow,
> My early visitation, and my last
> At even, which I bred up with tender hand
> From the first opening bud, and gave ye names!
> Who now shall rear ye to the sun, or rank
> Your tribes, and water from the ambrosial fount?
> Thee lastly, *nuptial* bower! by me adorn'd
> With what to sight or smell was sweet! from thee
> How shall I part?[38]

Yet many more numerous and more distinctive traces of Milton's angels than of his human beings lie fossilized in Melville's works.[39] One minor but clear-cut instance of this influence occurs in Melville's treatment of persons climbing the height of Mar Saba. He compares them to

> Uriel, warder in the sun,
> Who serious views this earthly scene
> Since Satan passed his guard and entered in.[40]

Here Melville must have had in mind the important role of Uriel in Books III and IV of *Paradise Lost*.[41]

Gabriel, Raphael, and Michael, however, are the angels of *Paradise Lost* which appear most significantly in Melville's works. He must often have thought of them as a trinity, for twice he wrote of them so:

I fancy that this mount [?] Shakespeare in heaven ranks with Gabriel, Raphael, and Michael.[42]

Your friends who have gone before are clearing out the seven-storied heavens, and making refugees of long-pampered Gabriel, Michael, and Raphael, against your coming.[43]

The fact that these are the three most prominent angels of the epic indicates that their association in this trinity is one groove which the poem worked in Melville's mind. Their Miltonic origin becomes even clearer when we inspect each in his independent appearances.

In *Mardi* Melville weaves one of his passages rich in proper nouns around the topic, "A king on his throne!" In part, it reads that

> Man lording over man, man kneeling to man, is a spectacle that Gabriel might well travel hitherward to behold; for never did he behold it in heaven. . . .
>
> A king on his throne! It is Jupiter nodding in the councils of Olympus; Satan, seen among the coronets in Hell.[44]

To us the mention of Jupiter certainly suggests pagan epics, and they in turn suggest the Christian epic which in many readers' minds glorifies Satan. From this use of *Paradise Lost* in the second paragraph just quoted, we can move backwards and explain the use of Gabriel in terms of associations with Satan. But in Melville's mind, as he wrote, the process may have been just the reverse. The search for a traveller from Heaven may have led to *Paradise Lost* as a catalogue of such persons, and that may have suggested the creation in the rhapsody of one paragraph using epic characters—those from earlier epics first, and then those from the later, English work. Certainly, to trace this reference to Gabriel back to *Paradise Lost* gathers justification from two later references to Gabriel in *Mardi,* for in one the connection with Milton is hardly to be questioned:

> Though Milton was a heretic to the creed of Athanasius, his faith exceeded that of Athanasius himself. . . .
>
> The higher the intelligence, the more faith, and the less credulity: Gabriel rejects more than we, but out-believes us all.
>
> West, West! West, West! . . . Hive of all sunsets!—Gabriel's pinions may not overtake thee![45]

Raphael, the second member of the trinity as first mentioned, has no Biblical existence outside the apocryphal Book of Tobit. He is, therefore, even more dependent on Milton for literary prominence than are Gabriel and Michael. Melville uses him to introduce a quotation in *The Confidence-Man* through the phrase,

Melville is echoing Milton's introduction of a unit of the dialogue between Raphael and Adam:

> To whom thus *Raphael* answer'd heavenly *meek.*[47]

Nineteen years after *The Confidence-Man*, Milton's Raphael reappeared with almost equal brevity in *Clarel:*

> If Eden's wafted from the *plume*
> Of shining Raphael, Michael palmy;
> If these in more than fable be,
> With natures variously divine—
> Through all their ranks they are masculine.[48]

The first line and a half of this passage is an extreme condensation of the following description of Raphael's shining arrival on earth, but with a typical adaptation of the material to Melville's immediate purpose—Milton's Raphael had wafted a fragrance which filled Paradise, whereas Melville's wafted a fragrance which suggested Eden:

> At once on the eastern cliff of Paradise
> He lights, and to his proper shape returns
> A Seraph wing'd: Six wings he wore, to shade
> His lineaments divine; . . .
>                                   the middle pair
> Girt like a starry zone his waist, and round
> Skirted his loins and thighs with downy gold
> And colours dipt in Heaven; the third his feet
> Shadow'd from either heel with feather'd mail,
> Sky-tinctur'd grain. Like Maia's son he stood,
> And shook his *plumes*, that heavenly fragrance fill'd
> The circuit wide.[49]

Years later Melville wrote a manuscript which he never published, a whimsical, sentimental sketch in which he asks, concerning the Marquis de Grandvin,

> Shall naught remain of his cherub sparkle and spirit?—nothing of all those ineffable qualities that make him what *Raphael*, Milton's *affable archangel*, would be seen to be were he commissioned hither to dissuade mankind from ever perpetrating an inhumanity or a pun?[50]

Here the recollection is exact, from

> Say, Goddess, what ensued when *Raphaël*
> The *affable Arch-Angel*, had forewarn'd
> Adam.[51]

Even more important in Melville's writing than either Gabriel or Raphael was the last of the trio, Michael. He appears in the Bible, though insignificantly, and in numerous literary and plastic uses. Therefore we cannot assume *a priori* that *Paradise Lost* is responsible for his prominence in Melville's mind. Fortunately there is evidence which proves the indebtedness to Milton.

On at least one occasion in addition to that recently discussed in the last passage on Eve, Melville used Michael in a phrase which recalls his role as prophet in the last two Books of *Paradise Lost:*

> Michael, the angel of truth, inspired me to write this to you on the instant.[52]

But to Melville, Michael was predominantly the warrior-leader of God's hosts, the Michael who looms large in Book VI of *Paradise Lost*.

This concept appeared first when Melville reviewed Parkman's *The California and Oregon Trail* for *The Literary World*. Parkman had noticed, in a frontier cabin, that

> a pistol loaded and capped, lay on the mantel-piece; and through the glass of the book-case, peeping above the works of John Milton, glittered the handle of a very mischievous-looking knife.[53]

In his review, Melville expanded the sentence just quoted into a humorous passage which shows typical actions of his creative mind. In the first place, it was like him to draw upon his knowledge of literature for colorful, filling detail. It was also normal for him to alter the facts as he found them in Parkman by moving the pistol from the mantelpiece to the books, perhaps because of too ready a reliance on memory. Finally, it was not unusual for him to lard the whole with humor:

> They visit a man in whose house is a shelf for books, and where they observe a curious illustration of life; they find a holster-pistol standing guard on a copy of Paradise Lost. We presume, then, that on our Western frontier, when a man desires to soar with Milton, he does so with his book in one hand, and a pistol in the other; which last, indeed, might help him in sustaining an "armed neutrality," during the terrible but bloodless battles between Captain Beelzebub and that gallant warrior Michael.[54]

That the battle in Book VI of the epic was terrible there can be little doubt; that it was bloodless hangs on one's interpretation of a symptom of Satan's wound:

> A stream of nectarous humour issuing flow'd
> Sanguine, such as celestial Spirits may bleed.[55]

In the year after the review of Parkman, Melville printed his regrets that

> seamen . . . continually behold a fellow-mortal flourishing over their heads like the archangel Michael with a thousand wings,[56]

and in writing the following comparison he probably had Michael in mind as the typical winged warrior:

> This simplicity renders a battle between two men-of-war, with their huge white wings, more akin to the Miltonic contests of archangels than to *the comparatively squalid* tussels of earth.[57]

There it is the presence of Michael that is almost certainly implied. In the following sentence from *The Piazza Tales* it is the presence of Milton that is implied with even greater clarity. This sentence speaks the cadence as well as the events of *Paradise Lost:*

> Either troops of shadows, an imperial guard, with slow pace and solemn, de-filed along the steeps; or, routed by pursuing light, fled broadcast from east to west—old wars of Lucifer and Michael.[58]

In *Clarel* Michael reappears, briefly, still as a warrior angel. A character is represented as

> hungering also for the day . . .
> When Michael's trump the call shall spread
> Through all your warrens of the dead.[59]

Milton had written that at the beginning of the war in heaven, "Michaël bid sound/ The Arch-Angel trumpet."[60]

It is *Battle-Pieces*, however, that contains Melville's most interesting use of Michael. Yet in order that one point in the discussion of *Battle-Pieces* may be clear when reached, we must first notice how several of the influences of style and description already analyzed separately, cooperate within part of the minor prose work "Cock-A-Doodle-Doo!"

The relevant passages, scattered in the original through thirteen pages of text, are these:

My eyes ranged over the capacious rolling country, and over the mountains, and over the village, and over a farmhouse here and there, and over woods, groves, streams, rocks, fells. . . .

I'd set [important villains and asses] to stokering in Tartarus. . . .

Here comes that old dragon [of a locomotive] again—that gigantic gad-fly of a Moloch—snort! puff! scream!—here he comes straight-bent through these vernal woods, like the Asiatic cholera cantering on a camel. Stand aside! here he comes, the chartered murderer! the death monopoliser! judge, jury, and hangman all together, whose victims die always without benefit of clergy. For two hundred and fifty miles that iron fiend goes yelling through the land, crying 'More! more! more!' Would that fifty conspiring mountains would fall atop of him! . . .

By the time that's drunk—a quart of stout—by that time, I shall feel about as stout as Samson. . . .

My soul, too, would . . . breathe forth a cheerful challenge to all the world of woes.[61]

The first of these sentences is Miltonic in its use of repetition and of a series, recalling through both its pattern and its words these lines:

> Through many dark and dreary vale
> They pass'd, and many a region dolorous,
> O'er many a frozen, many a fiery Alp,
> Rocks, caves, lakes, fens, bogs, dens, and shades of death.[62]

Next comes the mention of Tartarus, which has several times in this study appeared with Miltonic associations,[63] and which here precedes an ingenious comparison of a steam locomotive to Moloch. Three chief points of similarity are implied: fire, noise, and destruction. Only two of these, fire and destruction, could Melville have found in Biblical accounts of Moloch,[64] and although others than Milton may have informed him of the use of sound in the worship of the cruel deity,[65] an entirely adequate source is either of these passages of poetry, the first from *Paradise Lost*, the second from "On the Morning of Christ's Nativity," which Melville has already been shown to know well:

> First, Moloch, horrid king, besmear'd with blood
> Of human sacrifice, and parents tears;
> Though, for the noise of drums and timbrels loud,
> Their childrens cries unheard, that pass'd through fire
> To his grim idol.[66]

And sullen Moloch, fled,
Hath left in shadows dread
   His burning idol all of blackest hue;
In vain with cymbals' ring
They call the grisly king,
   In dismal dance about the furnace blue.[67]

One minor link which may have been tugging in Melville's mind is the blackness here ascribed to Moloch and very appropriate to a locomotive.[68]

In the same paragraph with the Moloch-locomotive comparison, Melville gives us examples of points of style already discussed as possibly parts of Milton's influence: poetic diction in "vernal airs,"[69] alliteration in "Asiatic cholera cantering on a camel," and an unusual compound in "death monopoliser."[70]

The next of the quotations from "Cock-A-Doodle-Doo!" contains not only a pun on two meanings of "stout," but a reference to Samson, whom Milton once described as evincing yet a third type of "stoutness."[71] Finally, Melville writes of "the world of woe," appearing to echo Milton's lines,

expell'd from hence into a world
Of woe and sorrow. . . .
That brought into this world a world of woe.[72]

In "Cock-A-Doodle-Doo!" phrases, stylistic peculiarities, and imagery from Milton have served Melville's sense of humor. In *Battle-Pieces*, however, there is occasion for the use of Milton but none for the presence of humor.

Melville's prefatory note to this first published volume of his verse states that

with few exceptions, the Pieces in this volume originated in an impulse imparted by the fall of Richmond. They were composed without reference to collective arrangement, but, being brought together in review, naturally fall into the order assumed.[73]

According to the first of these statements, most of the poems in *Battle-Pieces* were not written immediately after the events they memorialize—events of every year from 1859 to 1866. Instead, they were written between the fall of Richmond in 1865 and the publication of the book in 1866. According to the second of the quoted statements, the poems are independent of one another; the "order assumed" by those of the main part of the book is solely the chronology of the events described in the poems. Melville's opinion on the structure of the book greatly piques one's curiosity, for his use of symbolism drawn from Milton does give *Battle-Pieces* some degree of structure, as close analysis will show. The fact that all the poems were written within a few months will help to explain the consistency of the imagery.

The first two poems of *Battle-Pieces* deal with events of 1859 and 1860. The next poem, "The Conflict of Convictions," is dated "1860-1," and immediately precedes the first poem about the actual fighting. "The Conflict of Convictions" opens with this stanza:

> On starry heights
> A bugle wails the long recall;
> Derision stirs the deep abyss,
> Heaven's ominous silence over all.
> Return, return, O eager Hope,
> And face man's latter fall.
> Events, they make the dreamers quail;
> Satan's old age is strong and hale,
> A disciplined captain, gray in skill,
> And Raphael a white enthusiast still;
> Dashed aims, at which Christ's martyrs pale,
> Shall Mammon's slaves fulfil?

After five stanzas of mutually contradictory convictions about war, reform, and the mettle of the people, come these four lines of hope:

> Nay, but revere the hid event;
> In the cloud a sword is girded on,
> I mark a twinkling in the tent
> Of Michael the warrior one.[74]

As "The Conflict of Convictions" immediately precedes the poem which deals with the opening of the war at Fort Sumter, so "A Canticle" immediately follows the poem on the end of the war at Appomattox. "A Canticle" opens with these lines:

> O the precipice Titanic
> Of the congregated Fall,
> And the angle oceanic

77

Where the deepening Thunders call—
And the Gorge so grim
And the firmamental rim!

The next set of lines portrays the nation in victory and the Iris of its victory, but then Melville returns to

the foamy Deep unsounded,
And the dim and dizzy ledge
And the booming roar rebounded,
And the gull that skims the edge!
The Giant of the Pool
Heaves his forehead white as wool—
Toward the Iris ever climbing
From the Cataracts that call—
Irremovable vast arras
Draping all the Wall.[75]

In these two poems Melville is evidently writing of the Civil War in America with symbols from the civil war in Heaven, with some use of the fall of man. In the first of Melville's poems, "The Conflict of Convictions," "a bugle wails the long recall" of angels from the sight of "man's latter fall." The deep abyss of Hell is stirred with derision; her ruler, Satan, is strong and hale.[76] In much the same way Gabriel had led his band from Paradise after the fall of Adam and Eve, and Hell had been stirred with derision at that fall. Raphael is pictured largely as a cynic might see him in Milton— "a white enthusiast still,"[77] certainly not one of the greatest warriors in the celestial conflict. Christ's martyrs paled at the humanitarian aims which their leader had set them, and it is too much to hope that slaves of Mammon, "the least erected Spirit that fell/ From Heaven," will achieve such goals. America has already learned Mammon's habit of looking at pavements of trodden gold instead of at visions beatific.[78] Thus Melville's pessimistic view of his country on the threshold of civil war and his branding of masters as slaves is written through a symbolism markedly Miltonic, but also markedly altered into a passage that is Melville's, not Milton's.

Yet hope does exist in Melville's view. "In the cloud a sword is girded on," and there is a twinkling in the tent of Michael, the Lord's greatest general. Though one of the Northern champions may be a mere "white enthusiast," another is "the warrior one," and he is arming. The hope is justified. After the war, in "A Canticle," the deepening thunders of God's wrath are echoing over the rim of the firmament whence Satan's host has again fallen, over the congregated fall beneath the precipice Titanic. Satan, the Giant of the Pool, lifts his head to see the Iris of righteousness rising above irremovable cataracts hemming him within his foamy deep. "Thus Satan . . . / With head up-lift above the wave. . . ."[79]

Within the framework thus provided by "The Conflict of Convictions" and "A Canticle" are other poems whose Miltonic imagery, consistent with that just presented, both expands and affirms that of the two enclosing poems. Of particular importance are two which form a frame immediately within the larger one of "The Conflict of Convictions" and "A Canticle." "Apathy and Enthusiasm," the first of these, has already been referred to as the poem dealing with the opening of the war at Fort Sumter. In those days of Northern enthusiasm,

> the young were all elation
> Hearing Sumter's cannon roar,
> And they thought how tame the Nation
> In the age that went before.
> And Michael seemed gigantical,
> The Arch-fiend but a dwarf.[80]

Here more clearly than ever Michael is identified with the forces of the North, and Satan with those of the South. Melville was like most men of all times: he knew on which side God was fighting.

The subframe which is thus begun in "Apathy and Enthusiasm" is completed in "The Fall of Richmond." The former deals with the first fighting of the war, and immediately follows "The Conflict of Convictions." The latter deals with the last fighting in Melville's chronology, and, except for a short intervening poem on the surrender at Appomattox, immediately precedes "A Canticle." In "The Fall of Richmond" Melville is restrainedly exultant that his countrymen—Ulysses S. Grant standing for the archangel Michael —have won the war in Heaven:

> Hearts unquelled at last deter
> The helmed dilated Lucifer—
> Honour to Grant the brave.[81]

Enclosed by both sets of framing poems are two further references of the same type. At one point, having described a brave Confederate soldier, Melville comments that

> Such brave ones, foully snared
> By Belial's wily plea,
> Were faithful unto the evil end—
> Feudal fidelity.[82]

In another poem Melville writes of Northern soldiers going cheerfully to the early part of the war:

> No berrying party, pleasure wooed,
> No picnic party in the May,
> Ever went less loth than they
> Into that leafy neighborhood.
> In Bacchic glee they file toward Fate,
> Moloch's uninitiate.[83]

The young recruits were unwittingly going to a Moloch of fire and noise and death. The full horror which Melville intended us to find in "Moloch's uninitiate" is clearest to those who recall the Moloch of "Cock-A-Doodle-Doo!," of "On the Morning of Christ's Nativity," and of *Paradise Lost*.

Through these eight passages in which he referred to both the good and bad angels of *Paradise Lost* and in which, as the notes have shown, he often used Milton's words to describe them, Melville was able not only to suggest judgments about the conflicting armies, but also to give some unity to his collection of poems. Consciously or unconsciously using a technique of most partisan writers, he subtly bestowed the blessing of God on the soldiers whom he had wanted to see prevail. And consciously or unconsciously using a technique of which he does not hint in his prefatory note, he gives the main section of *Battle-Pieces* a structure beyond that of mere chronology.

80

# CHAPTER SIX

# THE INFLUENCE OF SATAN

> "—it being as true in literature
> as in zoology, that all life is
> from the egg."
> —The Confidence-Man, p. 319.

As might be expected, Melville had no faith that Satan is objectively real. In *Mardi* he indicated the vanity of believing "that evil is but permitted for a term; that for specified ages a rebel angel is viceroy,"[1] and in *Pierre* he remarked, "It is false, that any angels fell by reason of ambition. Angels never fall; and never feel ambition."[2] This attitude in no way interfered, however, with Melville's faith that Satan is artistically real, particularly as Milton portrayed him:

> There is no dignity in wickedness, whether in purple or rags; and hell is a democracy of devils, where all are equals. . . . Though Milton's Satan dilutes our abhorrence with admiration, it is only because he is not a genuine being, but something altered from a genuine original. We gather not from the four gospels alone any high-raised fancies concerning this Satan; we only know him from thence as the personification of the essence of evil, which, who but pickpockets and burglars will admire? But this takes not from the merit of our high priest of poetry; it only enhances it, that with such unmitigated evil for his material, he should build up his most goodly structure.[3]

Only a few years after this statement in *Redburn,* Melville asserted that Milton's Satan was one of the few greatly original characters of world literature.[4] Such praise, coupled with Melville's detailed knowledge of *Paradise Lost,* goes far towards explaining why Satan's influence is frequent in his works. Here again, however, we are dealing not with a tyrannical domination, but with a stimulating and provocative suggestiveness.[5]

81

Exclusive of those in *Moby-Dick*, there are about sixteen minor and relatively unrelated uses of Milton's Satan scattered from *Mardi* to *Clarel*. Some of them have already been mentioned—for example, Melville's references to Satan in *Battle-Pieces*. Others are either not significant enough to warrant discussion here,[6] or can be typified through two instances, the second of which is the more interesting.

To begin with *White Jacket*, Satan's biography there afforded Melville a means of magnifying the height of the royal yard of a line-of-battle ship: to fall thence is "almost like falling as Lucifer from the well-spring of morning down to the Phlegethon of night."[7] Seven years later, in *The Confidence-Man*, Melville used one of Milton's descriptions of Satan to help describe a snake and a human being, the cosmopolitan. Melville's borrowing makes the passage much more vivid for the general reader than it might otherwise be; for the reader who recalls the original in *Paradise Lost*, added horror is suggested, and the devilish nature of life aboard the *Fidèle* is re-emphasized:

> "I . . . am so eccentric as to have confidence in the latent benignity of that beautiful creature, the rattlesnake, whose lithe *neck* and *burnished maze* of tawny *gold*, as he *sleekly curls aloft* in the sun, who on the prairie can behold without wonder?"
>
> As he breathed these words, he seemed so to enter into their spirit—as some earnest descriptive speakers will—as unconsciously to *wreathe* his form and *side-long crest his head*.[8]

These words are taken from Milton's picture of Satan advancing to the temptation of Eve

> not with indented wave,
> Prone on the ground, as since; but on his rear,
> Circular base of rising folds, that tower'd
> Fold above fold, a surging *maze! his head*
> *Crested aloft*, and carbuncle his eyes;
> With *burnish'd neck* of verdant *gold* . . .
> . . . *side-long* he works his way,
> . . . and of his tortuous train
> *Curl'd* many a wanton *wreath* in sight of Eve. . . .
> Oft he bow'd
> His turret *crest*, and *sleek* enamell'd *neck*.[9]

Melville's minor uses of Satan are not, however, nearly so important as his uses of Satan in certain of his own leading characters —a subject which brings us to a consideration of Milton's influence on Melville's characterizations.

It has already been mentioned that Melville realized the difficulty of describing places and the value of suggestion in finishing such descriptions. He was equally aware of the difficulty of describing persons. In his first book, *Typee*, he admitted,

> I may succeed, perhaps, in particularising some of the individual features of Fayaway's beauty, but that general loveliness of appearance which they all contributed to produce I will not attempt to describe.[10]

In his last book, *Billy Budd*, Melville made a similar admission:

> Among the petty officers was one who, having much to do with the story, may as well be forthwith introduced. This portrait I essay, but shall never hit it.[11]

That the former quotation refers chiefly to a person's appearance, but the latter chiefly to a person's character may be significant of a shift in Melville's interest, but at any rate he found his knowledge of *Paradise Lost* valuable for both kinds of description.

Milton and Melville were alike not only in having fewer female characters than male, but also in believing that woman's chief glory is domestic rather than intellectual. The comparative rarity of female characters in his works limited Melville's opportunities for discussing the subject, but nothing in the rest of his writings contradicts the impression conveyed in *Clarel:*

> 'Twas not that Agar reasoned—nay,
> She did but feel, true woman's way. . . .
> To him [Clarel] now first in life was shown,
> In Agar's frank demeanour kind,
> What charm to woman may belong
> When by a natural bent inclined
> To goodness in domestic play.[12]

Agar was not, then, one of Milton's "fair female troop"

> empty of all good wherein consists
> Woman's domestick honour and chief praise.[13]

Melville's attitude in the matter is further revealed by a mark which he may have thought no one would ever bring into evidence— a pencil line beside this sentence addressed by Mrs. Percy Bysshe Shelley to Mrs. Gisborne and printed in *Shelley Memorials:*

83

In short, my belief is—whether there be sex in souls or not—that the sex of our material mechanism makes us quite different creatures; better, though weaker, but wanting in the higher grades of intellect.[14]

As we turn to Melville's _male_ characters we move to an area not only of much more significant parallels but also of much more clearly definable influences. Within this area let us approach Ahab through traits which link him to some of Melville's most prominent villains—Jackson, Bland, and Claggart.

Milton had implied in _Paradise Lost_, and stated in prose probably known to Melville,[15] that God gave Adam and his descendants reason as a guide to be followed in all their actions. Melville puts the same thought in the pen of Bardianna, and therefore in the mouth of Babbalanja:

> Undeniably, reason was the first revelation; and so far as it tests all others, it has precedence over them. It comes direct to us, without suppression or interpolation; and with . . . [God's] indisputable imprimatur.[16]

The common antithesis to reason is passion, and Milton as well as other authors[17] who may have influenced Melville in this matter recognized that although reason should be dominant, too often irrational drives overpower and enslave their rightful ruler. As Michael explains in _Paradise Lost_,

> Reason in man obscur'd, or not obey'd,
> Immediately inordinate desires,
> And upstart passions, catch the government
> From reason; and to servitude reduce
> Man, till then free. . . . He permits
> Within himself unworthy powers to reign
> Over free reason.[18]

When Melville used this dualism of the mind's forces in his characterizations, the result was men whose faculties of reason were enslaved by passions, whose monomanias lorded it over their powers of reasonable choice. Ahab and Claggart are the best examples.

> [Ahab's] great natural intellect, . . . that before living agent, now became the living instrument. If such a furious trope may stand, his special lunacy stormed his general sanity, and carried it, and turned all its concentrated cannon upon its own mad mark. . . . But that thing of his dissembling was only subject to his perceptibility, not to his will determinate.

Ahab himself confessed his case:

> I am madness maddened! That wild madness that's only calm to comprehend itself![19]

Claggart's symptoms are stated even more clearly:

> Though the man's even temper and discreet bearing would seem to intimate a mind peculiarly subject to the law of reason, not the less in his soul's recesses he would seem to riot in complete exemption from that law, having apparently little to do with reason further than to employ it as an ambidexter implement for effecting the irrational.[20]

Although neither of these men had been mastered by sensual appetite or conjugal fidelity, their situation was essentially the same as that of Adam and Eve in Book IX of *Paradise Lost*, for there may not be much to choose among the enemies of reason:

> Understanding rul'd not, and the Will
> Heard not her lore; both in subjection now
> To sensual Appetite, who from beneath
> Usurping over sovran Reason claim'd
> Superior sway.[21]

This Miltonic psychology may well have been important in causing Melville to create characters who were later described by the statement that

> whenever Melville wished to present human depravity he chose to make his villains—such as Jackson, Bland, Claggart—men of cold objectivity, not hot passion.[22]

Cold objectivity, then, not constant but usual, was one likeness between Melville's villains and Ahab on the one hand and Milton's Comus and Satan on the other. But there are other similarities as well.

The first of the trio of sea-going villains, Jackson, was so formidable and ugly "that Satan himself would have run from him," and his approach to death made it seem "as if he had indeed sold . . . [his soul] to Satan." Even more significant, a discussion of Jackson's wickedness prompted Melville to praise Milton's Satan in the important passage quoted in part on the first page of this chapter.

Interesting parallels of motivation and appearance supplement these explicit links. Redburn believed that one cause of Jackson's hatred for him was envy of his physical well-being: "For I was young and handsome, . . . whereas *he* was being consumed by an incurable malady, that was eating up his vitals." A similar case was that of the Belfast sailor who "was continually being abused and snubbed by Jackson, who seemed to hate him cordially, because of his great strength and fine person, and particularly because of his red cheeks."[23] Jealousy not very different from this was part of Satan's motivation too:

> The more I see
> Pleasures about me, so much more I feel
> Torment within me, as from the hateful siege
> Of contraries: all good to me becomes
> Bane. . . .
> Nor [do I] hope to be myself less miserable
> By what I seek, but others to make such
> As I, though thereby worse to me redound:
> For only in destroying I find ease
> To my relentless thoughts.[24]

In spite of such wickedness, some of Milton's readers pity his Satan as fully as Redburn pitied Jackson, and for much the same reason. In the novel, Redburn saw "even more woe than wickedness about the man; and his wickedness [seemed] to spring from his woe; and for all his hideousness there was that in his eye at times that was ineffably pitiable and touching."[25]

His eyes were apparently Jackson's most memorable feature, and on four occasions Redburn uses a snake or a serpent to describe them. In this he is not alone, for like earlier and later authors Melville often employs the suggestiveness of a snake or serpent in connection with villainy, sometimes with particular reference to eyes. Underlying the association in his mind may well have been Satan's use of the serpent of Paradise and his transformation into the greatest serpent of Hell. That link is almost explicit in the first of these instances, which is from *Moby-Dick:*

Short draughts [of grog]—long swallows, men; 'tis hot as *Satan's* hoof. So, so, it goes round excellently. It spiralizes in ye; *forks* out at the *serpent-snapping eye.*[26]

I watched Jackson's *eye* and saw it *snapping*, and a sort of going in and out, very quick, as if it were something like a *forked* tongue.[27]

Frescoes. Wags who painted them. *Tartarus*—tooth-pulling—*serpent* looking in *eye.*[28]

Bland, the most wicked character of *White Jacket*, bore the same mark: "Nothing but his mouth . . . and his *snaky*, black eye . . . betokened the accomplished scoundrel within." Like Satan, he evinced "intrepidity, coolness, and wonderful self-possession." These qualities were tested in him when he was convicted of crime, deprived of his rank, and forced to associate as an equal with the seamen whom he had victimized. Soon, however, he was accepted by most of them, for

> who can forever resist the very Devil himself, when he comes in the guise of a gentleman, free, fine, and frank? . . . I, for one, regarded this master-at-arms with mixed feelings of detestation, pity, admiration, and something opposed to enmity. I could not but abominate him when I thought of his conduct; but I pitied the continual gnawing which, under all his deftly donned disguises, I saw lying at the bottom of his soul. I admired his heroism in sustaining himself so well under such reverses.[29]

The latter part of this quotation parallels the pity for Jackson and Satan already mentioned; the disguise of sin recalls the wisdom of Adam and Satan that appeared when the former warned Eve "lest, by some fair-appearing good, [reason be] surpris'd," and when the serpent admitted the value of "hate stronger, under show of love well feign'd."[30]

Perhaps an even clearer hint of Satan is contained in White Jacket's conclusion that Bland "was an organic and irreclaimable scoundrel, who did wicked deeds as the cattle browse the herbage, because wicked deeds seemed the legitimate operation of his whole infernal organization."[31] The similarity is not to Milton's important theological justification of God in terms of freedom of the will, but to the serfdom of the will embodied in his characterization of Satan and expressed in Abdiel's penetratingly valid taunt of Lucifer,

Thyself not free, but to thyself enthrall'd.[32]

John Claggart exemplified the same thralldom. He suffered from "a depravity according to nature"; he had "no power to annul the elemental evil in himself."[33] And just as Jackson's roots in Milton's Satan were suggested by Melville's discussing Jackson in terms of Satan, in the same manner but with greater detail Claggart's share of the same literary ancestry is indicated. In two instances allusions clearly link Claggart to Satan: some of Claggart's actions are "caprices of the pit," and "what recourse is left to a nature like Claggart's, surcharged with energy as such natures almost invariably are, but to recoil upon itself, and, like the scorpion for which the Creator alone is responsible, act out to the end its allotted part."[34] In three other passages, allusions to Satan occur in explanations of circumstances which, with Claggart, are hostile to Billy Budd.[35] Finally, there is the heading of the second chapter analyzing the master-at-arms' character: "Pale ire, envy and despair."[36] These words Milton had used of Satan's emotions upon first sight of Eden;[37] Melville used them to introduce his analysis of Claggart's envy upon sight of Billy—and perhaps to hint at the cause of Claggart's pallor.[38]

Claggart's attitude towards the Handsome Sailor is much more complex than was Jackson's towards Redburn, and in that increased complexity it gains even more likeness to Satan's attitude towards man.[39]

> Claggart's was no vulgar form of [envy]. . . . If askance he eyed the good looks, cheery health, and frank enjoyment of young life in Billy Budd, it was because these happened to go along with a nature that, as Claggart magnetically felt, had in its simplicity never willed malice, or experienced the reactionary bite of that serpent. . . . One person excepted [,] the master-at-arms was perhaps the only man in the ship capable of adequately appreciating the moral phenomenon presented in Billy Budd, and the insight but intensified his passion, which at times assumed . . . [the form of] cynic disdain—disdain of innocence. To be nothing more than innocent! Yet in an æsthetic way he saw the charm of it, and fain would have shared it, but he despaired of it. . . .
>
> When Claggart's unobserved glance happened to light on belted Billy . . . , that glance would follow the cheerful sea-Hyperion with a settled meditative and melancholy expression, his eyes strangely suffused with incipient, feverish tears. . . . Yes, and sometimes the melancholy expression would have in it a touch of soft yearning, as if Claggart could even have loved Billy but for fate and ban.[40]

To the jealous hatred which Jackson evinced in *Redburn* and Satan in Book IX, there are here added not only a direct antithesis of good and evil, but also pity and potential love such as the earlier Satan felt towards Adam and Eve in Book IV of *Paradise Lost:*

> O Hell! what do mine eyes with grief behold! . . .
> Creatures of other mould,/ . . . whom my thoughts pursue

With wonder, and could love, so lively shines
In them divine resemblance, and such grace
The hand that form'd them on their shape hath pour'd. . . .
                    [I come] no purpos'd foe
To you, whom I could pity thus forlorn,
Though I unpitied. . . .
And should I at your harmless innocence
Melt, as I do, yet publick reason just,
Honour and empire with revenge enlarg'd,
By conquering this new world, compels me now
To do what else, though damn'd, I should abhor.[41]

Of course there are dissimilarities between this soliloquy and the previously quoted analysis of Claggart, but the common emphases on observed physical and spiritual beauty and on the apparent necessity for destroying what under some circumstances could be loved, far outweigh the differences.

Claggart has his similarities to Satan through the precedent of Bland as well as through that of Jackson.[42] Although his "incipient, feverish tears" come close to Redburn's admission that "there was that in [Jackson's] . . . eye at times that was ineffably pitiable and touching," they also hint at something like the "continual gnawing" inside Bland. They are the counterparts of the arch-villain's lament,

Me miserable! which way shall I fly
Infinite wrath, and infinite despair?[43]

Finally, Satan's and Bland's deceptive appearances are matched by Claggart's being "of no ill figure upon the whole," with "features, all except the chin, cleanly cut," and the aspect and manner of "a man of high quality, social and moral." His "occasional frank air and pleasant word went for what they purported to be, . . . [Billy Budd] never having heard as yet of the 'too fair-spoken man.' "[44] In the same way was Eve deceived.

The automatism of Claggart's evil, the serpent imagery of his book, the allusions to Satan and the quotation from Milton, the envy aroused by Billy's beauty of body and of character, the incipient love and actual suffering in Claggart's soul, and his misleading appearance determine his position as the ultimate development of Satanic villainy in Melville—that is if Ahab is no villain.

With no more than the usual accuracy of epigram, one might say

89

that in Claggart Melville reacted classically to Satan, whereas in Ahab he reacted romantically. In the former case he condemns a man who does wrong in the eyes of the world; in the latter he sympathizes with such a man, justifies his means by referring to his ends, and makes a hero of a devil. In *Billy Budd* his attitude towards Claggart is roughly analogous to that of Christ when he told God,

> Whom thou hat'st, I hate, and can put on
> Thy terrours, as I put thy mildness on,
> Image of thee in all things; and shall soon,
> Arm'd with thy might, rid Heaven of these rebell'd;
> To their prepar'd ill mansion driven down,
> To chains of darkness, and the undying worm;
> That from thy just obedience could revolt,
> Whom to obey is happiness entire.

In *Moby-Dick*, on the other hand, Melville's attitude towards Ahab is closer to that which Satan urged on Eve and for all mighty rebels:

> Will God incense his ire
> For such a petty trespass? and not praise
> Rather your dauntless virtue, whom the pain
> Of death denounc'd whatever thing death be,
> Deterr'd not from achieving what might lead
> To happier life, knowledge of good and evil?[45]

Admittedly this romantic attitude towards evil is not Milton's, and does injustice to *Paradise Lost.* It is, nevertheless, an attitude which Blake and Shelley had preceded Melville in holding, and which still has wide popularity. Melville was no more proof against being influenced by a misunderstanding than was the author of *Vulgar Errors* himself. Melville did not read Milton as do Douglas Bush and C. S. Lewis.[46] He read it with conceptions which led to his making Ahab one of the metamorphoses of Satan, and to his writing the following passage in which, only a year after the publication of *Moby-Dick*, Melville's romanticism shows itself in pity first for repented sin and then for unrepented sin:

Perfect Virtue does not more loudly claim our approbation, than repented Sin in its concludedness does demand our utmost tenderness and concern. And as the more immense the Virtue, so should be the more immense our approbation; likewise the more immense the Sin, the more infinite the pity. In some sort, Sin hath its sacredness, not less than holiness. And great Sin calls forth more magnanimity than small Virtue. What man, who is a man, does not feel livelier

90

and more generous emotions towards the great god of Sin—Satan,—than toward yonder haberdasher, who only is a sinner in the small and entirely honourable way of trade?[47]

The likeness between Satan and Ahab has not, of course, passed unnoticed. One critic writes,

Captain Ahab's character, in its relation to the supernatural expedition, is a composite of *all* the historical and mythical rebels against Destiny.[48]

*All* is probably an exaggeration, although *some* would not be, and Satan has several times been recognized as of the *some*. Carl Van Doren calls Ahab "the Yankee Faust, the Yankee Lucifer,"[49] and William Ellery Sedgwick believes that "Captain Ahab reminds us of Milton's Satan, of Prometheus, and thence, of Don Quixote."[50] Weber, a German scholar, is at greater length:

Melville's most interesting figure, Captain Ahab, shows all the depth and breadth of his vision. Without further ceremony we may place Ahab among the greatest creations of all literature; he has a peculiar kinship with them all, but especially with the Greek Prometheus and the Miltonic Satan. One cannot on that account speak of borrowing, for this fruit of the deep art of symbolism is a supreme literary achievement, such as succeeds spontaneously and for only the greatest artists at the height of their creative powers.[51]

Fortunately for the continuance of this study, Weber's "cannot ... speak of borrowing" may be balanced by Henry A. Murray's conclusion that "Captain Ahab, as grand a Satan as there is in literature, was America's contribution" to the Satan myth, which "can be traced from its distinguished progenitor in literature, Milton."[52]

A careful study of Captain Ahab soon reveals that, in addition to the quotations, verbal echoes, and stylistic similarities to *Paradise Lost* already noted, *Moby-Dick* contains numerous references and allusions to Milton's Satan—important hints and confirmations for our analysis of the Lucifer from Nantucket.

While looking for an inn in New Bedford, Ishmael came to a "smoky light" which lured him into a building where he first stumbled "over an ash-box" and then pushed open an inner door.

It seemed the great Black Parliament sitting in Tophet. A hundred black faces turned round in their rows to peer; and beyond, a black Angel of Doom was beating a book in a pulpit. It was a negro church; and the preacher's text was about the blackness of darkness.[53]

This is, of course, a bit of humor and not a declaration of literary indebtedness. To say so, however, does not answer the question of why Melville made merry in just these terms. Why, instead of Cornwall's grimy miners whom he used in *White Jacket* to suggest dwellers in darkness,[54] did Melville use Satan's Hell for that purpose in this early part of Ahab's story?

From New Bedford, Ishmael sails to Nantucket, where he and Queequeg put up at the Try Pots, before which hung

> a pair of prodigious black pots . . . ! Are these last throwing out oblique hints touching Tophet?[55]

As for Ahab himself, one side of his face and neck was scarred by a slender, livid mark which lightning had branded there.[56] In the case of Satan, "his face/ Deep scars of thunder had intrench'd."[57] A slender link, admittedly, but fortunately not alone. "Beelzebub himself," says Ishmael at one point, about whalers in general, "might climb up the side and step down into the cabin to chat with the captain, and it would not create any unsubduable excitement." Again, the *Pequod* sails off the Cape of Good Hope.

> Cape of Good Hope, do they call ye? Rather Cape Tormentoto, as called of yore; for . . . we found ourselves launched into this tormented sea, where guilty beings transformed into those fowls and these fish, seemed condemned to swim on everlastingly without any haven in store, or beat that black air without any horizon. . . . The silent ship . . . tore on through all the swift madness and gladness of the demoniac waves.

Not long after, Stubb is at some pains to convince Flask that Ahab's alter-ego, Fedallah, is the devil. Then Melville includes "the Devil" in a semi-serious list of "ponderous profound beings," and six pages later Ishmael described whales' tails:

> Out of the bottomless profundities the gigantic tail seems spasmodically snatching at the highest heaven. So in dreams have I seen majestic Satan thrusting forth his tormented colossal claw from the Flame Baltic of Hell.[58]

At intervals after this recall of the vivid opening scene of Milton's Book I, come a confession and two verbal links which particularly unite Ahab and the Satan of *Paradise Lost*. Ahab muses on the doubloon fastened to the mast of the *Pequod:*

> Look here,—three peaks as proud as Lucifer. The firm tower, that is Ahab, the

volcano, that is Ahab; the courageous, the undaunted, and victorious fowl, that, too, is Ahab; all are Ahab.[59]

Later Melville writes,

Let the unseen, ambiguous synod in the air, or the vindictive *princes* and *potentates* of fire, have to do or not with earthly Ahab, yet . . . he took plain practical procedures.[60]

Satan had once addressed his companions in fire as *"Princes, Potentates."*[61] In a later example, from "The Candles," Melville calls Ahab's harpoon a "fiery dart."[62] Michael had promised Adam

spiritual armour, able to resist
Satan's assaults, and quench his *fiery darts.*[63]

Near the close of "The Symphony," in which Ahab confesses himself "more a demon than a man," is a clear-cut reminder of *Paradise Lost* in the form of an apple of Sodom in a sentence already quoted:

But Ahab's glance was averted; like a blighted fruit-tree he shook, and cast his last, cindered apple to the soil.

Again, on the last day of the chase, Ahab muses in terms of the Creation,

What a lovely day again! were it a new-made world, and made for a summer-house to the angels, and this morning the first of its throwing open to them, a fairer day could not dawn upon that world.

On that very day, "Moby-Dick seemed combinedly possessed by all the angels that fell from heaven," and, when he had dealt his final, mortal blow, the *Pequod* sank. But as the ship went down, a sky-hawk, caught by Tashtego's hammer, went down with it.

And so the bird of heaven, with archangelic shrieks, and his imperial beak thrust upward, and his whole captive form folded in the flag of Ahab, went down with his ship, which, like Satan, would not sink to hell till she had dragged a living part of heaven with her, and helmeted herself with it.

Finally, and most impressive of all this series of evidence, is the Latin which Ahab "deliriously howled" as in the blood of his harpooners he tempered the harpoon destined for the White Whale:

Ego non baptizo te in nomine patris, sed in nomine diaboli.[64]

93

Four months before *Moby-Dick* was published Melville had written to Hawthorne,

> This is the book's motto (the secret one), *Ego non baptiso te in nomine*—but make out the rest yourself.[65]

On the basis of this chain of associations, the total of which is much stronger than the weakest link, we can have considerable confidence in the significance of more important but less obvious likenesses between the two heroes.

Coming, then, to the character of Satan and Ahab, we must remind ourselves again of the romantic criticism of *Paradise Lost*, and must see its applicability to *Moby-Dick*. For one matter, it is often difficult not to read into the grander moments of Ahab and Satan complete personal identification with Melville and Milton. Satan's eloquent speeches of resistance seem to have caught their fire from Milton's hatred of tyranny, and Ahab seems autobiographical not only in the practice of whaling but also in initiative of intellect. Obviously Milton did not think of Satan as representing an ideal way of life, nor did Melville so think of Ahab, yet some persons interpret both characters as representing the perfection of human nature. In this case Milton's creation is probably more grossly misread than Melville's for at least the latter did intend that Ahab be the hero of his book. More important than any such difference, however, is the fact that both books can be read—whether intelligently or not is another question—as the stories of great and almost wholly admirable rebels akin to Prometheus. This attitude we shall need to keep in mind.

The root of greatness and of woe, for Satan and for Ahab, was pride.[67] Their creators both mention the tragic flaw and have their characters acknowledge their own *hubris*. On the one hand Melville comments that "in his fiery eyes of scorn and triumph, you then saw Ahab in all his fatal pride," and Ahab soliloquizes, "Here I am, proud as Greek god."[68] On the other hand, Milton writes of Satan's

> baleful eyes . . .
> Mix'd with obdurate pride and stedfast hate,

while Satan speaks his hatred of those beams

94

> That bring to my remembrance from what state
> I fell, how glorious once above thy sphere;
> Till pride and worse ambition threw me down.[69]

C. S. Lewis has noted that "the stock response to Pride, which Milton reckoned on when he delineated his Satan, has been decaying since the Romantic Movement began."[70] Melville's pity of Ahab links him somewhat with that decay, though he saw clearly enough that pride is evil. And he saw as clearly as Milton did that it is a motive to one of the greatest crimes, the greatest that Satan and Ahab are guilty of—sacrilege. The proud person, believing that he deserves treatment appropriate to his self-inflated dignity, is quick to anger when he receives a less welcome treatment. At the exaltation of the Messiah, Satan

> could not bear
> Through pride that sight, and thought himself impair'd.

Satan's first speech in Hell includes mention of his "sense of injur'd merit."[71] Ahab's story presents different details—chief of them Moby-Dick's biting off his leg—but the same psychological pattern, the same thought that spiritually as well as physically he has been impaired, the same sense of injured merit. Then Satan's defeat in Heaven made him less than angel, as Ahab's loss of his leg made him less than man. When the two of them were tormented by

> the thought
> Both of lost happiness and lasting pain,[72]

the hurts to their pride irked fully as much as the hurts to their bodies. Earlier than the opening actions of *Paradise Lost* and *Moby-Dick*, were actions in which Satan and Ahab had assailed the order of the universe. Inevitably they had been repelled and punished. But that experience, instead of breeding in them respect for superior forces—such regard as Belial learned and Starbuck knew—bred only a spirit of vengeance which, to justify and to encourage itself, refused to see the moral and physical superiority of its opponent.

It is true that if any pride is ever justifiable, a case could be made to justify some of the pride of Satan and Ahab. In their courage, skill, and acumen they were not entirely unworthy opponents of omnipotence. Perhaps the outstanding evidence of their superiority

95

to the ordinary run of men and of angels is their dominance of their fellows together with the fact that some of their fellows were not easily dominated. With a show of winning the free consent of their followers, Satan and Ahab actually impose their wills in tyrannical fashion.[73] That they are able to do so in spite of the opposition they face merely augments our respect for their ability and our abhorrence of their lack of morality. Satan maintained the loyalty of all his other followers despite the open and spirited defection of Abdiel; with the help of Beelzebub he swerved to his own ends the council of Pandemonium despite the eloquence of Moloch, Belial, and Mammon. Ahab met his Abdiel in Starbuck, yet this was an Abdiel who lost heart, who soon confessed to himself, "I plainly see my miserable office,—to obey, rebelling; and worse yet, to hate with touch of pity!"[74]

The fatal pride which scorned all the *nicht-Ich* did not, however, give either its clearest or its most damning manifestation in a tyranny which carried subordinates to ruin. It showed most clearly and most damnably in the sacrilege already mentioned. Addison called Satan's a "proud and daring Mind which could not brook Submission even to Omnipotence,"[75] and a student of Melville has it that in Ahab's case as well as others, "the Titanism of the mind, the mind's refusal to admit its mortal limitations in its pursuit of the Ultimate, implies a denial of any force higher than itself, a denial of God."[76] Such sacrilege is greater than that implied in Elijah's talk, either of Ahab's "deadly scrimmage with the Spaniard afore the altar in Santa," or of "the silver calabash he spat into." Ahab's greatest sacrilege comes in such speeches as his soliloquy in his cabin:

Ay! I lost this leg. I now prophesy that I will dismember my dismemberer. Now, then, be the prophet and the fulfiller one. That's more than ye, ye great gods, ever were. I laugh and hoot at ye, ye cricket-players, ye pugilists, ye deaf Burkes and blinded Bendigoes! I will not say as schoolboys do to bullies,—Take some one of your own size; don't pommel *me!* No, ye've knocked me down, and I am up again; but *ye* have run and hidden. Come forth from behind your cotton bags! I have no long gun to reach ye. Come, Ahab's compliments to ye; come and see if ye can swerve me. Swerve me? ye cannot swerve me, else ye swerve yourselves! man has ye there. Swerve me? The path to my fixed purpose is laid with iron rails, whereon my soul is grooved to run. Over unsounded gorges, through the rifled hearts of mountains, under torrents' beds, unerringly I rush! Naught's an obstacle, naught's an angle to the iron way![77]

96

Such disdain of omnipotence smacks partly of the fierce urgings and defiances of Moloch, whose

> trust was with the Eternal to be deem'd
> Equal in strength; and rather than be less
> Car'd not to be at all.

It is also of the essence of Satan's ambition to "erect his throne Equal" to God's. Satan too had "trusted to have equall'd the Most High," and even after his fall had hopes of "maistring Heav'n's Supreme."[78]

Starbuck saw clearly enough the evil which he could not successfully resist. To Ahab himself he said, "To be enraged with a dumb thing, Captain Ahab, seems blasphemous." Ahab answered, "Talk not to me of blasphemy, man; I'd strike the sun if it insulted me." Starbuck could only meditate, "Ay, he would be a democrat to all above. . . . His heaven-insulting purpose, God may wedge aside."[79]

Interestingly enough, it is not merely against Ahab's moral character that Starbuck protests. He protests also against Ahab's conduct of the practical affairs of the voyage. Time after time he impresses upon Ahab the rights of the *Pequod's* owners; he acts as the watchdog of financial gain. As such he contributes to the impression that part of the rich design of *Moby-Dick* is Ahab's revolt against the hierarchy of capitalism, or at least against the deification of practicality. If men of Milton's day found their restraining duty in God, men of Melville's day found theirs in property. Ahab was as much an exception to the latter pattern as Satan was to the former. Yet it is, near the surface at least, the former pattern involving God, with Ahab's revolt against it, which is dominant in *Moby-Dick*. All this is not to deny that

> the White Whale swam before . . . [Ahab] as the monomaniac incarnation of all those malicious agencies which some deep men feel eating in them, till they are left living on with half a heart and half a lung. That intangible malignity which has been from the beginning; to whose dominion even the modern Christians ascribe one-half of the worlds; which the ancient Ophites of the East reverenced in their statue devil;—Ahab did not fall down and worship it like them; but deliriously transferring its idea to the abhorred White Whale, he pitted himself, all mutilated, against it. All that most maddens and torments; all that stirs up the lees of things; all truth with malice in it; all that cracks the sinews and cakes the brain; all the subtle demonisms of life and thought; all evil, to crazy Ahab, were visibly personified, and made practically assailable in Moby-Dick.[80]

97

May it be after all that the whale, not Ahab, is a metamorphosis of Satan, whereas Ahab is an agent of God? Melville would have it that St. George was a whale-hunter; is Ahab a spiritual as well as professional re-embodiment of the Saint? Were both Ahab and Michael representing moral power combatting mere physical force represented by the White Whale and by Satan? Possibly we are on the brink of an ambiguity in which the distinction between good and evil is as difficult to make as it is again and again in *Pierre*. More probably, however, a path leads away from ambiguity. Perhaps the path can be found in John Freeman's statement that in Melville's own mind the evils which Ahab saw in the whale "are subdued to a metaphysical view or half-view of the world, but in . . . Ahab they are freed and enlarged into domination."[81] A hatred of evil grows so great that it is no longer a virtue; it becomes an evil to which Ahab sacrifices his own virtues and the lives and souls of his crew. A good impulse becomes a monomania; or, to return to the psychology of Milton, Pope, and Melville, a passion potentially virtuous becomes a Master Passion of such tremendous force that it emerges a blasphemous, sacrilegious power. It takes to itself God's function of overcoming the devil, and becomes so absorbed in the struggle that it forgets the existence of God—it even comes to think of itself as the equal of God.[82] As Melville wrote in the passage most recently quoted from *Moby-Dick*, "crazy" Ahab "deliriously" transferred to the White Whale the idea of intangible malignity. Ahab maligned the whale as wrongfully as Satan maligned God.

Yet to find the faults of Ahab is not to erase the great fault of Moby-Dick, brutality. If the White Whale is a symbol for any God of western culture, it must be for the Jehovah of the Old Testament, for God as a primitive force, not as a father of mankind, not even as the power who talked in the garden with Adam.[83] The White Whale is not amiable to the reader no matter how many leagues of mind separate the reader from Ahab. On the other hand, Ahab has traits which the reader admires to a greater or less degree. Out of this situation arises the fact that "without altering the orthodox outcome of the strife of a man with Heaven, Melville has nevertheless managed to make the rebel, with all his sins, the nobler of the antagonists. . . . Though he will not be bullied

98

*ambiguity*

by force, Ahab would kneel to deity made manifest in love.[84]

Surely our admiration for Ahab is not merely negative, based on a dislike of his antagonist or on a belief that Ahab is a trifle less repulsive than that antagonist. We may say that the White Whale seemed more evil to Ahab than it really was, just as God seemed less good to Satan than he really was. We may say that both Ahab and Satan exaggerate the evil in what they hate, that both under-value their opponents' strength and so persuade themselves to assail *yes.* the unconquerable, and that both fight forces with which most of us would say they have no real quarrel. But the feeling remains that

> rightly to be great
> Is not to stir without great argument,
> But greatly to find quarrel in a straw  √
> When honour's at the stake.[85]

Foolish as that romantic attitude may be, it forms the stuff of many great stories, and the exaltation of Messiah or the loss of a leg can prove a sufficient straw to some natures. Then revenge must be taken. Soon after his fall from Heaven, Satan's

> care
> Sat on his faded cheek, but under brows
> Of dauntless courage, and considerate pride
> Waiting revenge.

*depends on your point of view - pride + stupidity*

But later, just before the fall of man, he acknowledged that

> Revenge, at first though sweet,
> Bitter ere long, back on itself recoils.[86]

That wisdom is also Melville's and is applied to Ahab: *

> Ah, God! what trances of torment does that man endure who is consumed with one unachieved revengeful desire. *like Satan*

The moral judgments of Satan and of Ahab which have appeared thus far really involve a question not yet raised in connection with Ahab alone—freedom of will. If he chose his own fatal pride and his own want of responsibility, then he is to blame for the motiva-tion and for the effect of his actions; but if they were thrust upon him, he is as innocent as an assassinating bullet. Ahab himself seems rather clearly to believe that he is "the Fates' lieutenant," acting "under orders." "What is it," he asks, √

*× L*

99

what nameless, inscrutable, unearthly thing is it; what cozening, hidden lord and master, and cruel, remorseless emperor commands me; that against all natural lovings and longings, I so keep pushing, and crowding, and jamming myself on all the time? . . . By heaven, man, we are turned round and round in this world, like yonder windlass, and Fate is the handspike.[87]

This might seem like a trumped up necessity, "the tyrant's plea,"[88] were it not that Melville seems to confirm Ahab's self-analysis, saying of him, as he was to say of Claggart, that Ahab was "without power to kill, or change, or shun the fact" of his dissembling, which "was only subject to his perceptibility, not to his will determinate." For Melville's considered opinion on free will, we should probably look to its metaphorical intertwining with fate and chance in "The Mat-Maker,"[89] but so far as Ahab is concerned, there seems to have been little possibility of the captain's determining his own purposes on the *Pequod's* last voyage. In the same way, the fate that dominated Satan seems to have been a stronger one than that recognized by Milton's theology.

Ahab and Satan deserve our pity, however, whether they are complete masters of themselves or not. They are unhappy, and are completely aware of their unhappiness; they are marked by the "continual gnawing" which marked Jackson, Bland, and Claggart.[90] Of Satan approaching Paradise we read,

> Horrour and doubt distract
> His troubled thoughts, and from the bottom stir
> The Hell within him; for within him Hell
> He brings, and round about him nor from Hell
> One step, no more than from himself, can fly
> By change of place.

Then Satan himself laments,

> Me miserable! which way shall I fly . . . ?
> Which way I fly is Hell; myself am Hell;
> And, in the lowest deep, a lower deep
> Still threatening to devour me opens wide.[91]

Strikingly in the same vein are these lines about Ahab:

When, as was sometimes the case, these spiritual throes in him heaved his being up from its base, and a chasm seemed opening in him, from which forked flames and lightnings shot up, and accursed fiends beckoned him to leap down among them; when this hell in himself yawned beneath him, a wild cry would be heard through the ship.[92]

100

Only for a few moments is the inner torment of these men relieved. Once the sight of Eve so charms Satan that

> That space the Evil-one abstracted stood
> From his own evil, and for the time remain'd
> Stupidly good; of enmity disarm'd
> Of guile, of hate, of envy, of revenge.[93]

Once on a "clear steel-blue day," when the sky was "pure and soft, with a woman's look"—when an Eve of air charmed him—Ahab also stood abstracted, "faint, bowed, and humped." He talked with Starbuck of their wives and children in Nantucket, helping to fill a chapter called "The Symphony."[94] But for neither character does the spell last long. The hell that always burned within Satan "soon ended his delight,"[95] and Ahab soon "shook, and cast his last, cindered apple to the soil."[96] The psychology of Milton's character suffers no more than a sea-change before it molds this Yankee Lucifer.

In these mutual inner hells, distinguishing flames mark some of the mutual woes. For one matter, each protagonist suffers at the perception of pleasures not for him. After his brief enchantment by Eve, Satan's "hot Hell"

> . . . tortures him now more, the more he sees
> Of pleasure not for him ordain'd.

He had earlier confessed,

> the more I see
> Pleasures about me, so much more I feel
> Torment within me, as from the hateful siege
> Of contraries: all good to me becomes
> Bane.[97]

Ahab, watching a sunset from his cabin window, feels the same torture:

> This lovely light, it lights not me; all loveliness is anguish to me, since I can ne'er enjoy. Gifted with the high perception, I lack the low, enjoying power; damned, most subtly and most malignantly! damned in the midst of Paradise![98]

A second identifiable woe is the chagrin which Satan and Ahab feel at the means they must use. Their pride is hurt. Satan, planning to enter the serpent's body, laments his "foul descent"—a descent particularly foul for one who "to the highth of Deity aspir'd."

But what will not ambition and revenge
Descend to? Who aspires, must down as low
As high he soar'd; obnoxious, first or last,
To basest things.[99]

Ahab could learn that lesson no better than Satan. While the carpenter worked at a new ivory leg for him, Ahab stormed,

Here I am, proud as Greek god, and yet standing debtor to this blockhead for a bone to stand on! Cursed be that mortal inter-indebtedness which will not do away with ledgers. I would be free as air; and I'm down in the whole world's books.[100]

Then too there was loneliness, which, like sacrilege, is often a child of pride. The master of the *Pequod* saw it:

Ahab stands alone among the millions of the peopled earth, nor gods nor men his neighbors! Cold, cold—I shiver!

This loneliness was more than the mere fact that "socially, Ahab was inaccessible,"[101] and had its roots in his spirit as well as in the ritual of command. Both Milton and his character perceived the same penalty of pride, and Satan too regretted it.[102]

A further cause of unhappiness to Satan and Ahab was their concern for their followers. Never a major absorption, never strong enough to turn the leader from the path of pride, this interest was, nevertheless, of some importance to these predominantly self-centered beings. It is true that both led their followers into conspiracy against supreme power, asserting their superiorities of intellect and personality to override the dissenting voices of a Starbuck, an Abdiel, and then a Belial or Mammon. But perhaps a more striking similarity lies in their occasional regard for the welfare of their underlings. Good leaders in the heroic tradition that they were, neither Ahab nor Satan asked a follower to take more risks than he himself took. Just as Satan arranged to do the scouting towards Earth himself, taking all the risk—and hoping for all the glory—so Ahab labored that his boat might be the foremost in the fight against the White Whale. Furthermore, the first words spoken in *Paradise Lost* are Satan's to Beelzebub:

If thou beest he; but O, how fallen! how chang'd
From him, who, in the happy realms of light,
Cloth'd with transcendent brightness, didst outshine
Myriads though bright!

102

Later, as he was about to address his armies, Satan's eye cast

> Signs of remorse and passion, to behold
> The fellows of his crime . . . condemn'd
> For ever now to have their lot in pain. . . .
> Thrice he assay'd [to speak], and thrice, in spite of scorn,
> Tears, such as Angels weep, burst forth.[103]

The same sympathy is Ahab's; Captain Peleg was not wrong in telling Ishmael that "stricken, blasted, if he be, Ahab has his humanities." Even this salt-caked sea-dog refrained from patrolling the quarterdeck so that his mates might sleep, and in "The Symphony" he felt so strongly drawn to Starbuck that he sought to save him from a premonitioned doom, commanding him to keep the ship when Moby-Dick is lowered for.[104]

These were the common inner woes that Satan and Ahab felt as they pushed their conflicts with almightiness. Reverses met them outwardly. The Ahab who surveyed the wreckage of his boat and the affliction of his crew relived the experience of the Satan who surveyed the fiery lake of Hell with

> baleful eyes
> That witness'd huge affliction and dismay
> Mix'd with obdurate pride and stedfast hate.

Yet neither seamen bobbing in the landless Pacific nor angels overwhelmed in floods of tempestuous fire could quell the spirits of these leaders. With a single voice they ask,

> Till then who knew
> The force of those dire arms? Yet not for those,
> Nor what the potent victor in his rage
> Can else inflict, do I repent or change,
> Though chang'd in outward lustre, that fix'd mind,
> And high disdain from sense of injur'd merit,
> That with the Mightiest rais'd me to contend. . . .
> What though the field be lost?
> All is not lost; the unconquerable will,
> And study of revenge, immortal hate,
> And courage never to submit or yield,
> And what is else not to be overcome;
> That glory never shall his wrath or might
> Extort from me. To bow and sue for grace
> With suppliant knee, and deify his power,

> Who from the terrour of his arm so late
> Doubted his empire; that were low indeed,
> That were an ignominy, and shame beneath
> This downfall.[105]

Yet these words of sacrilegious pride are spoken before the last, greatest reverse of all, in which a parallel irony underlines the power of the enemy they fought: as an apple had been Satan's weapon against Eve, so an apple climaxed his doom in Hell; as the harpoon line had been part of Ahab's weapon against the White Whale, so that harpoon line wrought his doom in the chase—the third day.

Both Satan and Ahab were hurt in their great pride by powers which they might seem to harm, but could never destroy. Rallying ill-fated followers to their impious revolts, they war against invincibility with which they have no real quarrel. The pursuit of such proud revenge, urged home in spite of danger and futility, is perhaps but a human manifestation of superhuman forces. Perhaps in each there is control by fate, an inner destiny which puts new meaning in Starbuck's thrust, "Let Ahab beware of Ahab, beware of thyself, old man."[106] But whether they are free agents or not, we are forced to admire their fortitude and sympathy, and to pity them for their inner suffering and their loneliness. Theirs was an inner dynamism compounded not entirely of Hell. Theirs was a consanguinity immeasurable but sure.

104

*He — the King
who angered
God so much*

# CHAPTER SEVEN

# THE FINAL HARVEST

*"I have now finish'd my Observations
on a Work which does an Honour to
the English Nation."*
—*Addison on* Paradise Lost *in
the* Spectator, *No. CCCLXIX.*

THE bulk of the evidence concerning Melville's opinion of Milton
has already been entered in this case, for imitation probably expresses more esteem than does any other action. "The gods had
much rather mankind should resemble than flatter them."[1] It is
possible, however, to be somewhat more precise than we have yet
been about the specific kind and degree of esteem involved.

One important type of testimony yet untapped is the markings
made by Melville in the extant volumes of his library. A study of
these markings is, in a sense, a continuation of the subject already
discussed in part of Chapter I—Milton's popularity in America
and his fame in Melville's circle. There the emphasis was on the
American reflections of Milton which helped to shape the environment of Melville's formative years. Now, on the other hand, we
must examine English books which Melville read after the writing
of his major prose—after 1859.[2]

Melville's marginal pencillings have yet to be exhaustively
studied, but a survey of all that are available demonstrates that in
almost every case, pleasure from or agreement with a given passage
is indicated by underlining or by a check or vertical line in the
margin. In contrast, disagreement is indicated by written comments. Even if this is true, there is not, of course, much significance to be gathered from every marking. When he read Elizabeth

105

Barrett Browning's "Casa Guidi Windows," Melville lined two passages dealing with Milton's supposed pleasure at seeing Vallombrosa,[3] but important conclusions are hard to draw in this instance. The same is true of a comment in Joseph Forsyth's *Remarks on Antiquities . . . in Italy*. Forsyth had written that

> English poets cannot plead for the sonnet one successful precedent. Even the greatest of them all, Shakespeare, Milton, Spenser, split on this rock and sank into common versifiers.

Melville rejoined,

> What pedantry is this! Yet its elegance all but redeems it. Forsyth is the most graceful of pedants.[4]

This certainly decides something about Melville's attitude towards pedantry, but whether it shows his thoughts on the sonnet or even on one of these sonneteers is far from certain.

Somewhat more to the point, although not yet conclusive, are three judgments by Edmond Scherer and one by Dr. Johnson, all four of which Melville checked while reading Arnold's "A French Critic on Milton." Scherer is quoted to the effect that "Luther and Calvin, those virtuosos of insult, had not gone further" than did Milton in his prose, and that when he writes an epic, Milton "will bequeath to us a poem which is at once the most wonderful and the most insupportable in existence." The third judgment that Melville marked was Scherer's summary of Milton:

> Elegant poet and passionate disputant, accomplished humanist and narrow sectary, admirer of Petrarch, of Shakespeare, and hair-splitting interpreter of Bible-texts, smitten with Pagan antiquity and smitten with the Hebrew genius; and all this at once, without effort, naturally; an historical problem, a literary enigma!

The dictum from Johnson is the famous one: "Surely no man could have fancied that he read Lycidas with pleasure had he not known the author!"[5] All of these contain something less than hearty praise of Milton. Perhaps Melville marked the sentences because he agreed with the detraction; perhaps he merely delighted in the iconoclasm.

Certainly most of the comments on Milton which he lined contained praise of the poet. Melville knew "L'Allegro" and "Il Penseroso" well, and used them in his own writing. It is hardly surprising, therefore, that he checked Scherer's comment that these poems are marked by "nothing morose or repellent, [but by] purity without excess of rigour, gravity without fanaticism."[6] Similarly consistent with Melville's knowledge and use of *Areopagitica* is his having marked passages on and from that work in Disraeli's *Curiosities of Literature*.[7]

It was stated in Chapter I that Melville read largely for confirmation, and additional evidence for that assertion can be found in his markings of criticisms of *Paradise Lost.* One sentiment to be confirmed was that already quoted from *Redburn*, that Satan is Milton's "most goodly structure" and "dilutes our abhorrence with admiration."[8] In Shelley, Melville found confirmation from a high authority, confirmation which was sure to appeal to a romantic reader of *Paradise Lost* and to the creator of Captain Ahab. When Melville came to these sentences in the "Defence of Poetry," his pencil followed his eye:

> Milton's poem contains within itself a philosophical refutation of that system, of which, by a strange and natural antithesis, it has been a chief popular support. Nothing can exceed the energy and magnificence of the character of Satan as expressed in "Paradise Lost." . . .
>
> This bold neglect of a direct moral purpose is the most decisive proof of the supremacy of Milton's genius.

This much was marked with but one line, however. Two lines expressed even greater enthusiasm for Shelley's dictum:

> Milton's Devil as a moral being is as far superior to his God, as one who perseveres in some purpose which he has conceived to be excellent in spite of adversity and torture, is to one who in the cold security of undoubted triumph inflicts the most horrible revenge upon his enemy.

*nonsense*

It is important to note that Melville was approving Shelley's criticism in the midst of an environment which accepted praise of Milton's orthodoxy from Hester Mulso Chapone and William Ellery Channing. Apparently, then, Melville read Milton in a way different from that of many of his contemporaries. He could not accept the Milton praised by piety, but he did accept the Milton who had been accepted and explained by Blake and Shelley. It was the latter kind of Milton that influenced *Moby-Dick*, that made a hero of a Satan and a villain of a God. Between passages which Melville marked, Shelley had written that Milton's God

107

inflicts the most horrible revenge upon his enemy, not from any mistaken notion of inducing him to repent of a perseverence in enmity, but with the alleged design of exasperating him to deserve new torments.

Does not the Whale exasperate Ahab to the same end? And Shelley also writes,

Implacable hate, patient cunning, and a sleepless refinement of device to inflict the extremest anguish on an enemy, these things are evil; . . . although redeemed by much that ennobles his defeat in one subdued.[9]

The application of this passage to Ahab is unmistakable. From that application we should not conclude that Shelley influenced Melville, but we should see clearly that Melville thought of *Paradise Lost* in the way of the most romantic tradition—a tradition which is embodied in *Moby-Dick*. This being so, the inner affinity which Melville felt for Milton was even greater than was earlier indicated. Instead of that affinity's being checked by intellectual disagreements, it was enlarged by intellectual concord.

In addition to Shelley, the second important critic for whom we have Melville's reactions is Matthew Arnold. As he read "On Translating Homer," the American prose poet marked his interest in the grand style by lining these passages and the italicized words:

When Milton says:
> "His form had yet not lost
> All her original brightness, nor appeared
> Less than archangel ruined, and the excess
> Of glory obscured,"—

That . . . is in the grand style. . . . Dante has [produced a body of poetry in the true grand style], and so has Milton: and *in this respect Milton* possesses a distinction which even *Shakespeare*, undoubtedly the supreme poetical power in our literature, does not share with him. Not a tragedy of Shakespeare but contains passages in the worst of all styles, *the affected style*. . . . In spite, therefore, of objections which may justly be urged against the plan and treatment of the Paradise Lost, in spite of its possessing, certainly, a far less enthralling force of interest to attract and carry forward the reader than the Iliad or the Divine Comedy, it fully deserves, it can never lose, its immense reputation; for, like the Iliad and the Divine Comedy, nay in some respects to a higher degree than either of them, it is in the grand style.[10]

Other markings indicate that Melville was well aware of the formal complexity of Milton's developed style. He underlined a comment by Arnold on "the inversion and pregnant conciseness"

108

of Milton, and lined the statement that "between Cowper and Homer there is interposed the mist of Cowper's elaborate Miltonic manner."[11] The latter quotation is remarkably similar to a phrase which Melville underlined in a letter from Coleridge to Wordsworth: "Cowper's *cumbersome most anti-Homeric Miltonism.*" That phrase he ran across in an Introduction to Chapman's Homer. In the same volume he underlined Chapman's "*Up* from the grey sea *like a cloud,*" and wrote in a note, "Exhalation     Milton—'rose like an exhalation'—the Ponderous form."[12]

It appears, then, that Melville liked not only to read Milton, but to read about him. He enjoyed those critics who recognized that Milton was not without flaws, and he appreciated emphasis on the heroism of Satan and on "the Ponderous form."

When Melville wrote about Milton he sometimes recorded the hearty praise already quoted from his novels. At other times he mingled his praise with some of the youthful, American exuberance which Emerson had shown in writing that "perhaps Homer and Milton will be tin pans yet."[13] Melville checked and underlined Burns's familiar "Jock Milton" in the "Poem on Pastoral Poetry";[14] and in his own "Hawthorne and His Mosses" he hip-hoorahed,

> We want no American Goldsmiths: nay, we want no American Miltons. It were the vilest thing you could say of a true American author, that he were an American Milton. Call him an American and have done, for you cannot say a nobler thing of him.

Before publication Melville changed the second *Milton* to *Tompkins.*[15] Was his motive deference to American esteem of Milton, or to his own respect for the poet? In any event, it is interesting that the first *Milton* was allowed to stand, apparently as a symbol for the peak of British poetic achievement.

Again, the havoc which time wreaks on all literature, including Milton's works, impressed Melville, as when he lined Shelley's prophecy:

> The Divina Commedia and Paradise Lost have conferred upon modern mythology a systematic form; and when change and time shall have added one more superstition to the mass of those which have arisen and decayed upon the earth, commentators will be learnedly employed in elucidating the religion of ancestral Europe, only not utterly forgotten because it will have been stamped with the eternity of genius.[16]

109

Another havoc, wreaked on literary esteem by the practical affairs of life, appeared in *White Jacket:*

> After all, though "Paradise Lost" be a noble poem, and we man-of-war's men, no doubt, largely partake in the immortality of the immortals; yet, let us candidly confess it, shipmates, that, upon the whole our dinners are the most momentous affairs of these lives we lead beneath the moon.[17]

The importance of such half-humorous remarks lies, of course, not in what they state, but in what they imply. When Melville wished to use a name that conjured up the notion of poetic greatness, he frequently used either the name of Milton's epic or of its author.

Perhaps a trifle more significant of Melville's real esteem for Milton is the remark, in an allusion-studded passage of *Mardi*, that "blind Milton sings bass to my Petrarchs and Priors."[18] Here *bass* seems to carry a compliment, suggesting profundity and deep worth which contrast with the superficiality of the alliterating Petrarch and Prior. Of equal suggestiveness is a comment in the review of Parkman's *California and Oregon Trail*. Why should we condemn savages? Melville asks. "Xavier and Elliot despised not the savages; and had Newton or Milton dwelt among them they would not have done so."[19] The choice of Newton and Milton is a rather odd one for this context. The best explanation would seem to be that these names were selected to suggest the finest scientific and poetic intellects known to Melville and his audience.

That explanation is rendered yet more plausible by reports of Melville's lecture "Statuary in Rome." According to one account of the lecture, "The elevating effect of such statues [as the *Apollo Belvedere*] was exhibited in the influence they exerted upon the mind of Milton during his visit to Italy."[20] According to a summary of a repetition of the lecture, Melville "described the various statues and groups of the Vatican, the streets, churches and private palaces of Rome, and referred to the description of Milton as 'a Vatican done into verse.'"[21] The important aspect of these reports is not so much the justification which Melville had for his statements about Milton,[22] as it is the emphasis which he and the reporters gave to this poet alone. The reporters' summaries were brief; Melville must have made much of Milton in the lecture, or the reporters must have found Milton more familiar than other of Melville's materials.

110

Evidently Melville fitted into the contemporary pattern of Milton-worship, with the exception that Melville was sure, as his coevals were not, to distinguish between Milton the poet and Milton the religious leader. Melville rejected the latter at the same time that he lauded the former, being careful to make the laudation explicit, while the rejection remained only implicit.

But then one is tempted to try to carry the matter a little further and to inquire where Melville ranked Milton in the hierarchy of English poets. After the only important land-based friendships in Melville's life—those with Duyckinck and Hawthorne—had passed their peaks during the 1850's, "Melville was left to consort with the ghosts of men who had died hundreds of years before—they alone . . . affording him that sense of spiritual affinity which he sought vainly in the universe of the living." But who his favorite ghosts were, and in what order he ranked them, can never be certainly determined. Stanley Geist would put Shakespeare at the head of them,[23] whereas Nathalia Wright holds that of all Melville's prose "catalogues of, and references to, authors, books, characters, events, legends, and fables, . . . most distinct and most consistent . . . are the Biblical allusions."[24] To Shakespeare and the Bible Milton should probably in this case defer, but to no third.

While discussing genius in "Hawthorne and His Mosses" Melville himself cites Shakespeare as "the very greatest example on record."[25] This must, however, be reconciled with the already quoted statement that Milton is "our high priest of poetry."[26] The two remarks were published within eleven months of each other[27]—a sufficient interval in which to change one's mind, of course. But "high priest" may have been used simply to indicate that Milton is the finest religious poet we have. In any event, it is certain that on two occasions Melville did use Milton as a symbol of the very highest type of originality. Once he mentioned him alone, and once he linked him with Shakespeare and Cervantes. The former instance is in *Pierre:*

> The world is forever babbling of originality; but there never yet was an original man, in the sense intended by the world; the first man himself—who according to the Rabbins was also the first author—not being an original; the only original author being God. Had Milton's been the lot of Caspar Hauser, Milton would have been as vacant as he.[28]

111

The flow of associations here from Adam through authorship to Milton is of course not to be overlooked. In the second instance, in *The Confidence-Man*, Melville introduced a lengthier discussion of originality in these words:

> As for original characters in fiction, a grateful reader will, on meeting with one, keep the anniversary of that day. True, we sometimes hear of an author who, at one creation, produces some two or three score such characters; it may be possible. But they can hardly be original in the sense that Hamlet is, or Don Quixote, or Milton's Satan.[29]

Jaunty as he sometimes was about Milton, Melville clearly recognized and acknowledged that in the poet there had operated a creative intellect which deservedly stood, for Melville and his readers, as a symbol of artistic greatness. Melville may or may not have thought Milton the greatest English poet, and he may or may not have been influenced more by Milton than by any other author. Yet certainly Melville is the only major American author to have been influenced by Milton to a significant degree. Though Melville may not have praised Milton as fulsomely as did Emerson and Lowell, he paid Milton the compliment of a much fuller indebtedness.

Some of the statistics of that indebtedness look small enough at first glance. Twelve mentions of the poet, six mentions of his characters, three of scenes in his works, and thirteen quotations—this total of thirty-four is not large. But it contains only the incontrovertible instances, those of which there can be no doubt. If we then add the probable quotations from Milton, the almost certain allusions to Miltonic characters, the hardly questionable debts to Miltonic scenes and ideas, and the passages which are all but surely paraphrases or verbal echoes of Milton, we bring the total number of citations up to one hundred and thirty-four.[30] The compilation of such a number has its values as well as its faults if we look to it for significant comment.

In the first place, the compilation can show the extent to which *Paradise Lost* outweighed the other sources of Miltonic influence. One hundred and four passages were based on the epic, whereas only thirty came from Milton's life, prose, and minor poems. The one hundred and four are scattered with remarkable evenness through all Books of the epic except the shortest, Book VII, which contributed much less than did any of the others.

In the second place, the citations are distributed with surprising evenness throughout the course of Melville's career, from "Fragments from a Writing-Desk" to *Billy Budd*. As one might expect, the longest works—*Mardi*, *Moby-Dick*, and *Clarel*—have the greatest number of citations, and one hazards the guess that if *Clarel* had not been written in its own strangely crabbed style, it would have shown many more obvious Miltonic influences. Nevertheless, its total of thirteen indebted passages, compared with sixteen for *Mardi* and a like number for *Moby-Dick*, suggests the even pulse of Milton's influence during Melville's career. Most of his sources he used once, and used no more.

In the generally even distribution of the Miltonic passages lies part of the answer to the question of when Melville read or reread Milton's works. The fact that almost three-fourths of the passages were written between 1845 and 1857 is hardly significant, for those years gave us over three-quarters of Melville's publications, journals, and letters. Nor is the sudden burst of citations at the time of *Mardi* conclusive of anything relevant to this question. The figures of two citations from *Typee* and one from *Omoo*, but sixteen from the next book, loom large only until one reflects on the greater length of *Mardi* and, more importantly, on the much richer texture of that book. The jump from one to sixteen is further evidence that to explain some aspects of *Mardi* one must weigh three possibilities: Between *Omoo* and *Mardi* Melville read so much that he unconsciously reflected his reading in his writing; between *Omoo* and *Mardi* Melville found delight in authors like Milton who made a show of learning, and consciously imitated them; between *Omoo* and *Mardi* Melville thought of so much to say that he had to increase the warp and woof of his prose if it were to bear his meaning. Certainly absence of reference to an author before *Mardi* is no evidence of unfamiliarity with him, just as mention in *Mardi* is no proof that Melville had more than heard of him. Nevertheless, two bits of evidence, when combined, make it seem a little more than possible that Melville's first reading of *Paradise Lost* came in 1847 or 1848, when he was working on *Mardi*. One point is that, of the six pre-*Mardi* uses of Milton, the two that are unquestionably Miltonic are from "L'Allegro," not *Paradise Lost*. The other point is a statement of questionable

113

accuracy, in *Redburn*, that a chant heard in Liverpool produced the same effect upon Melville that his "first reading of Milton's 'Invocation to the Sun' did years afterward."[31] "Years afterward," written of 1837 when Melville was in Liverpool, would hardly suggest any date earlier than 1844, when Melville left the sea. But then, "first reading" implies a second reading before *Redburn* appeared in 1849. The first reading may well have come in 1847 or 1848, when Melville was beginning to educate himself as a man of letters.

Finally, the tabular break-down of the figure "one hundred thirty-four" outlines the extent to which Milton added fulness of detail to Melville's works, supplemented his memory as a source of their contents, and facilitated his thinking about human nature and literary art.

But statistics can by no means tell all the story. "One hundred thirty-four" does not, for instance, emphasize the fact that some of the quotations appear in such informal sources as letters, journals, and marginal jottings, indicating what might be termed the private presence of Milton in Melville's mind. Nor does "one hundred thirty-four" point out that Melville's journals, the best place to look for intimate knowledge, contain more quotations and allusions from Milton than from any other author. "One hundred thirty-four" does not reveal the inaccuracy of some of the quotations. At times his inaccuracy suggests that Melville wrote hastily, with a desire to give chiefly the aroma of learnedness, and with a memory well enough stocked with Miltonic lore to feel independent of reference books[32] or learned friends. On some occasions,[33] however, Melville's inaccuracies can be laid to his conscious or unconscious fusing of two Miltonic passages.

Bare statistics fail also to bring out the fact that although "Had Milton's been the lot of Caspar Hauser" is a not very significant comment, the criticism of Milton's Satan in *Redburn* and *The Confidence-Man*, voiced as it is while novels stand still, is evidence of considerable reflection—a condition favorable to influence. Numbers cannot be expected to tell of the variety in Melville's use of his source. At times he was consciously, if humorously, ostentatious in his use of *Paradise Lost*, as in the "Extracts" preceding Chapter One of *Moby-Dick*. Sometimes his probably conscious

114

allusions to *Paradise Lost* add overtones, as grandeur and demonism are suggested at the sinking of the *Pequod*, "which, like Satan, would not sink down to hell till she had dragged a living part of heaven along with her, and helmeted herself with it." In other instances Melville was probably unaware of the associative richness given his prose when, from his deep well of reading unconsciously recalled, he described the *Pequod* as "a noble craft, but somehow a most melancholy," or described Ahab's harpoon as a "fiery dart."[34]

If these matters cannot be handled through addition and subtraction, we must cast aside all numbers when we try to summarize Milton's influence on other aspects of Melville's style and on his handling of Jackson, Bland, Claggart, and Ahab. A part of Melville's style is marked by phrases hauntingly Miltonic: "Well, be it hell. I will mould a trumpet of the flames, and, with my breath breathe back my defiance!"[35] Or another example: "some gigantic condor, floating at brooding poise on outstretched wings."[36] Although such phrases have no significant verbal parallels in Milton, one can point to a generally iambic rhythm and to a Miltonic use of vowel sounds. These are Miltonic echoes. The number of Melville's repetitions, cumulations, *-ean* adjectives, inversions, suspensions, omissions, parentheses, substitutions of parts of speech, words from poetic diction, series of proper nouns, unusual compound words, sonorous passages and passages of dignity, iambic rhythms and epic similes—how many of these were sown by Milton we know not and no search can make us know. Their indeterminable total represents, however, one of the two major influences of *Paradise Lost*, and so of Milton, on Melville's works.

The other major influence is that of Satan. Through allusions and references to Milton's hero, Melville gave three of his important characters stature in evil-doing, gave them a dignity and prominence which was to compensate for their lowly environments and make these products of democratic literature equal to the titled villains of older, aristocratic works. As Melville expressed the problem once, "even though . . . this Yankee Jackson . . . was a nameless vagabond without an epitaph," he must be accounted "full as dignified a personage as [Tiberius] . . . , and as well meriting

115

his lofty gallows in history."[37] In a parallel fashion Melville used hints of Satan to add "high qualities, though dark; . . . tragic graces; . . . some ethereal light" to the "Nantucket grimness and shagginess" of the "poor old whale-hunter," Ahab.[38] But Melville does more than vaguely hint that Ahab is as great as Satan. He gives him the qualities that created Satan's greatness.

Milton's influence on Melville will be one of the major factors of that book, if ever written, which covers the whole road to Albemarle, which covers all of Melville's reading and its effects. Milton's influence is one of those which caused Melville to pay tribute to the past, and pleasure found in Milton was a contributing cause of Melville's allowing his characters the joys of books. This influence was one large product of that fondness for reading which took Melville to the libraries of the frigate *United States*, of Evert Duyckinck, of the New York Society, and of second-hand dealers in America and Europe. Many references in his works, many qualities of his style, many facets of his characterization came to Melville in part because he passed his formative years in a society full of Milton's accomplishment, but even more because that soil of environment was fertilized by an inner affinity. And yet in no sense are we guilty of the fault which Melville hinted at when he wrote that "imitation is often the first charge brought against originality."[39] In this case imitation can be neither the first nor the last charge. Like the other great writers of our culture, Melville used the past, but only to build upon it with an artistry which set it in new luster, remolding beauty for the readers of a newer age.

# APPENDICES

In the appendices the following abbreviations are used for Melville's works, here arranged in chronological order:

| | |
|---|---|
| *FWD* | "Fragments from a Writing-Desk" |
| *T* | *Typee* |
| *O* | *Omoo* |
| *M* | *Mardi* |
| *R* | *Redburn* |
| *WJ* | *White Jacket* |
| *J* | *Journal of a Visit to London and the Continent* |
| *MD* | *Moby-Dick* |
| *P* | *Pierre* |
| *CADD* | "Cock-A-Doodle-Doo!" |
| *E* | "Encantadas" |
| *TT* | "Two Temples" |
| *IP* | *Israel Potter* |
| *HF* | "Happy Failure" |
| *POB* | "Paradise of Bachelors" |
| *JR* | "Jimmy Rose" |
| *IAMC* | "I and My Chimney" |
| *ATT* | "Apple-Tree Table" |
| *Pi* | "Piazza" |
| *CM* | *Confidence-Man* |
| *JUS* | *Journal up the Straits* |
| *BP* | *Battle-Pieces* |
| *C* | *Clarel* |
| *JM* | *John Marr* |
| *Tim* | *Timoleon* |
| *Ppo* | Posthumous poetry |
| *Ppr* | Posthumous prose |
| *BB* | *Billy Budd* |

# APPENDIX A

Melville's copy of Milton either does not exist, or exists unknown to scholars, yet it is almost unbelievable that for many decades there did not stand on Melville's shelves an edition of at least Milton's poetry, marked, annotated, and well-worn. Melville's familiarity with Milton's poems and the lack of any record that he ever purchased or borrowed an edition of Milton, impel the conclusion that he long possessed his own copy of this favorite author, just as he possessed copies of the Bible, Shakespeare, Jonson, Burton, Browne, and others whose pages he relished.

Numerous editions of Milton's poetry were, of course, available for inclusion in Melville's library. Only a few surmises are possible concerning which he owned; the chief one is based on a letter which he wrote in Boston in 1849:

> I am mad to think how minute a cause has prevented me hitherto from reading Shakespeare. But until now, any copy that was come-atable to me, happened to be in a vile small print unendurable to my eyes which are tender as young sparrows. But chancing to fall in with this glorious edition, I now exult over it, page after page. . . . It is an edition in glorious great type, every letter whereof is a soldier, & the top of every "t" like a musket barrel.[1]

Melville needed a Milton also in large type. His grandfather's copy, which was "come-atable" to him, would have ruined his eyes.[2] But which of the numerous available large-type editions did Melville own? Two are suggested by evidence at best far from conclusive.

In the first place, there was Hilliard, Gray, and Company's edition. In 1837 this Boston firm had published the Shakespeare "in glorious great type," Melville's copy of which is now in the Houghton Library.[3] In the previous year the same firm had reissued an equally well printed two-volume edition of Milton's poetry.[4] Both editions by Hilliard, Gray, and Company can be further tied to Melville by an interesting though weak link. On the spines of all volumes of Melville's Shakespeare, and on the title-pages of both volumes of the Milton, is stamped the Aldine printer's mark of a dolphin encircling an anchor. Precisely such a mark in precisely those locations provided grist for *Moby-Dick:*

As for the bookbinder's whale winding like a vine-stalk round the stock of a descending anchor—as stamped and gilded on the backs and title-pages of many books both old and new—that is a very picturesque but purely fabulous creature.[5]

In the second place there are reasons for believing that Melville's Milton was the edition from which the quotations in this study have been taken, Todd's second edition of *The Poetical Works of John Milton*, published in London in 1809 in seven volumes. This edition has as legible lines as does the Hilliard, but has also the advantage of far more copious notes. In them and in Todd's "Life and Writings of Milton," printed in Volume I of the edition, Melville may have found some material used in his own works, as is mentioned in the notes to the present study.[6] Todd also provided a Verbal Index which may have been useful to Melville.

And yet it may have been a very different, third edition that Melville used. "The dead, blind wall butts all inquiring heads at last."[7]

# APPENDIX B

This appendix contains supplementary evidence for points made in Chapter III.

## BRIEF PARAPHRASES

1. "Gentle gales" occurs in *FWD*, XIII, 388, in an invocation which immediately precedes the quotation from "L'Allegro." Cf. *P.L.*, IV, 156.
2. *M*, I, 36: "The grisly king," referring to death.
   *P.L.*, IV, 821: "The grisly king," referring to Satan.
3. *M*, II, 352, 355: weal or woe
   *P.L.*, VIII, 638, etc.: weal or woe
4. *R*, p. 169: Bob Still . . . enthrones himself in the sentry-box, *holding divided* rule *with* thy spouse.
   *P.L.*, IV, 110–111:                         By thee at least
                    *Divided* empire *with* Heaven's King I *hold.*
5. *WJ*, p. 245: dragged them *down with* him to *the same destruction* with *himself*
   *S.A.*, 11. 1657–1658: Samson, *with* these immix'd, inevitably
                    Pull'd *down the same destruction* on *himself.*
6. *WJ*, p. 500: with *brooding darkness* on the face of the deep
   "L'Allegro," 1. 6: Where *brooding Darkness* spreads his jealous wings.
7. *MD*, I, 15: swift destruction
   *P.L.*, V, 907: swift destruction

8. *P*, p. 51: Touch her not, ye airy devils; hence to your appointed hell! why come ye *prowling* in these *heavenly purlieus?*

     *P.L.*, II, 832–833:    [Earth is] a place of bliss
                        In the *pourlieus* of *Heaven.*

           IV, 183:    [Satan leaping into Paradise is like] a *prowling* wolf.

9. *P*, p. 404: On that ivory-throned brow, old Saturn cross-legged sat.

     *P.L.*, II, 1, 5:  High on a throne . . . Satan exalted sat.

     cf. *M*, I, 151:  Old Aaron . . . cross-legged sat.

10. *E*, X, 249:  upon the scorching marl

     *P.L.*, I, 296:  over the burning marle

11. *CM*, p. 172:  To what *vicissitudes* of *light and shade* is man subject!

     *P.L.*, V, 643–644:  that high mount of God, whence *light and shade*
                           Spring both

        VI, 5–8:                      the mount of God . . .
            Where *light* and darkness in perpetual round
            Lodge and dislodge by turns, which makes through Heaven
            Grateful *vicissitude*, like day and night.

12. *CM*, p. 198:  *Circling wiles* and bloody lusts

     *S.A.*, 1. 871:  where all thy *circling wiles* would end

13. *BP*, p. 25:  shagged with brush

     *Comus*, 1. 429:  shagg'd with horrid shades

14. *BP*, p. 55:  But where the sword has plunged *so deep,*
                And then been turned within the *wound*
                By *deadly Hate,* . . .
                Shall North and South their rage deplore,
                And reunited thrive amain
                Like Yorkist and Lancastrian?

     *P.L.*, IV, 98–99:        For never can true reconcilement grow,
              Where *wounds* of *deadly hate* have pierc'd *so deep.*

15. *BP*, p. 95:  *Necessity the plea*

     *P.L.*, IV, 393–394:  *necessity,/ The* tyrant's *plea*

16. *BP*, p. 101:  of endless date

     *P.L.*, XII, 549:  of endless date

17. *BP*, p. 163:  As when brave *numbers without number*, massed.

     *P.L.*, III, 345–346:  The multitude of Angels, with a shout
                     Loud as from *numbers without number.*

18. *BP*, p. 184:  Courage and fortitude matchless

     "To the Lord General Cromwell," 1. 3:
                 Guided by faith and matchless fortitude.

     [Note how Melville out-Miltons Milton by using a postpositional adjective.]

19. *C*, I, 191:  Fair *Circe*—goddess of the *sty*

     *Comus*, 11. 50, 77:  On *Circe's* Island fell . . .
                   To roll with pleasure in a sensual *sty.*

20.  *C*, I, 273:   A champion of true liberty—
                  God's liberty for one and all—
                  Not Satan's licence.
     "I did but Prompt the Age," 1. 11:
                  Licence they mean when they cry liberty.

21.  *C*, I, 309:   *Coasting* inquisitive the *shore*
                  And frequent stooping
     *Comus*, 1. 49:   *Coasting* the Tyrrhene *shore*
     *P.L.*, III, 71:  *Coasting* the wall of Heaven

22.  *C*, II, 173:          Vine and Rolfe remained
                  *At gaze*; the soldier too and Druze.
     *P.L.*, VI, 205–206:   Nor stood *at gaze*
                  The adverse legions.

23.  *Tim*, p. 260:   Beaming spears and helms salute
                  The *dark with bright*.
     *P.L.*, III, 380:  *Dark with* excessive *bright* thy skirts appear.

24.  *Ppr*, p. 121:   So Orme pursued his solitary way.
     *P.L.*, XII, 649:   Through Eden took their solitary way.
     [Note the similar rhythms.]
     cf. *R*, p. 277:   plodding my solitary way to the same old docks

25.  *Ppo*, p. 342:   In harbinger airs how we freshen,
                  When, clad in the *amice* of *gray* silver-hemmed
                  Meek coming in twilight and dew,
                  The *Day-Spring*, with pale, priestly hand and begemmed,
                  Touches, and coronates you.
     *P.R.*, IV, 426–427:   Thus passed the night so foul, till Morning fair
                  Came forth, with pilgrim steps, in *amice gray*.
     *P.L.*, V, 139; VI, 521; *S.A.*, 1. 11:   Day-Spring
See also Postpositional Adjectives.


# POETIC DICTION

| | | |
|---|---|---|
| Afric | *P.L.*, I, 585, etc.* | *MD*, I, 309, etc. |
| amain | *P.L.*, II, 165, etc. | *MD*, I, 299. |
| aright | *P.L.*, VI, 470, etc. | *MD*, II, 226, etc. |
| asphaltic | *P.L.*, I, 411, etc. | *MD*, I, 9. |
| bosky | *Comus*, 1. 313. | *MD*, I, 36. |
| clime (climate) | *P.L.*, I, 242, etc. | *O*, p. 77. |
| eld | "Death of a Fair Infant," 1. 13. | *Tim*, XVI, 293, etc. |
| emergent | *P.L.*, VII, 286. | *FWD*, XIII, 395. |
| emprise | *P.L.*, XI, 642, etc. | *MD*, II, 219. |
| erst | *P.L.*, I, 360, etc. | *M*, II, 276, etc. |
| fain | *S.A.*, 1. 1535, etc. | *MD*, I, 16, etc. |
| finny | *Comus*, 1. 115. | *MD*, II, 111. |

121

| glebe | *P.R.*, III, 259. | *M*, II, 306. |
| hap | *P.L.*, IX, 160, etc. | *MD*, I, 70. |
| hapless | *P.L.*, II, 549, etc. | *O*, p. 37. |
| haply | *P.L.*, I, 203, etc. | *M*, I, 2. |
| ken | *P.L.*, I, 59, etc. | *M*, II, 377. |
| lave | *P.R.*, I, 280, etc. | *MD*, II, 252. |
| magnific | *P.L.*, V, 773, etc. | *Ppo*, XVI, 395. |
| meads | "L'Allegro," 1. 90, etc. | *MD*, I, 129. |
| meet (fitting) | *P.L.*, III, 675, etc. | *MD*, II, 252. |
| nigh | *P.L.*, I, 700, etc. | *MD*, I, 15, etc. |
| ope | *P.L.*, XI, 423, etc. | *M*, II, 347, etc. |
| passing (very) | *P.L.*, XI, 717, etc. | *MD*, I, 330. |
| plight | *P.L.*, I, 335, etc. | *MD*, I, 9, etc. |
| puissant | *P.L.*, I, 632, etc. | *MD*, I, 136. |
| reck | *P.L.*, II, 50, etc. | *M*, II, 355. |
| supernal | *P.L.*, I, 241, etc. | *MD*, II, 282. |
| verdant | *P.L.*, IV, 697, etc. | *MD*, I, 349, etc. |
| ween | *P.L.*, IV, 741, etc. | *MD*, II, 34, etc. |
| whilome | *Comus*, 1. 827, etc. | *M*, II, 342. |
| wight | *P.L.*, II, 613, etc. | *MD*, I, 77, etc. |
| wondrous | *P.L.*, I, 703, etc. | *MD*, I, 237, etc. |
| wonted | *P.L.*, I, 527, etc. | *CM*, p. 176, etc. |
| ycleped | "L'Allegro," 1. 12 | *M*, I, 305. |
| yon | *P.L.*, I, 180, etc. | *MD*, I, 15, etc.† |

*\*Etc.* here indicates one or more further occurrences in the same or other works by each author.

†Perhaps this list should include *amaranthine* (*Pierre*, p. 477, etc.; *P.L.*, XI, 78). Raymond Dexter Havens includes it among many "words in *Paradise Lost* that would have sounded unusual to the average intelligent reader of the late seventeenth or early eighteenth century" (*Influence of Milton*, pp. 83–84). Sundermann has noted it, in connection with a song in *Clarel* (II, 70), as "a symbol of immortality (Homer), . . . of which Milton also sang" (*Melvilles Gedankengut*, p. 139).

## COMPOUND WORDS

The columns, from left to right, contain Milton's words, Melville's words, sources for the former, and sources for the latter.

### ADJECTIVE PLUS ADJECTIVE

| timely-happy | gloomy-jolly | "How soon hath time," 1. 8. | *MD*, II, 165. |
| aery-light | deep-heady | *P.L.*, V, 4. | *P*, p. 360. |

### ADJECTIVE PLUS NOUN

| swart-star | wild-ocean | "Lycidas," 1. 138. | *MD*, I, 309. |

122

## ADJECTIVE PLUS PARTICIPLE

| | | | |
|---|---|---|---|
| wide-water'd | ready-roasted | "Il Penseroso," 1. 75. | *M*, I, 40. |
| sable-vested | green-turfed | *P.L.*, II, 962. | *MD*, I, 316. |
| civil-suited | mystic-marked | "Il Penseroso," 1. 122. | *MD*, II, 32. |
| slow-endeavouring | soft-cymballing | "Shakespeare," 1. 9. | *MD*, II, 230. |
| empty-vaulted | strange-thoughted | *Comus*, 1. 250. | *MD*, II, 240. |
| deep-vaulted | deep-loaded | *P.R.*, I, 116. | *MD*, II, 243. |
| wide-wasting | wide-slaughtering | *P.L.*, VI, 253. | *MD*, II, 270. |
| half-rounding | half-wheeled | *P.L.*, IV, 862. | *MD*, II, 275. |
| full-orb'd | flat-faced | *P.L.*, V, 42. | *MD*, II, 337. |
| high-climbing | devious-cruising | *P.L.*, III, 546. | *MD*, II, 368. |
| wide-encroaching | wide-expanded | *P.L.*, X, 581–582. | *HF*, XIII, 213. |

## ADVERB PLUS PARTICIPLE

| | | | |
|---|---|---|---|
| long-wander'd | long-skirted | *P.L.*, XII, 313. | *MD*, II, 40. |
| seventimes-wedded | fore-announced | *P.L.*, V, 223. | *MD*, II, 44. |
| divinely-warbled | darkly-tanned | "On the Morning of Christ's Nativity," 1. 96. | *MD*, II, 196. |
| fourfold-visag'd | forward-flowing | *P.L.*, VI, 845. | *MD*, II, 364. |
| cross-flowing | down-coming | *Comus*, 1. 832. | *MD*, II, 364. |
| over-labour'd | over-arboured | *S.A.*, 1. 1327. | *JR*, XIII, 257. |

## NOUN PLUS ADJECTIVE

| | | | |
|---|---|---|---|
| snow-soft | whale-wise | "Death of a Fair Infant," 1. 19. | *MD*, I, 289. |
| virtue-proof | God-omnipresent | *P.L.*, V, 384. | *MD*, II, 169. |
| star-proof | fathom-deep | "Arcades," 1. 89. | *MD*, II, 212. |
| tongue-doughty | life-restless | *S.A.*, 1. 1181. | *MD*, II, 213. |
| crop-full | death-glorious | "L'Allegro," 1. 113. | *MD*, II, 366. |
| sun-bright | glory-immortal | *P.L.*, VI, 100. | *ATT*, XIII, 315. |

## NOUN PLUS NOUN

| | | | |
|---|---|---|---|
| love-tale | life-spot | *P.L.*, I, 452. | *MD*, I, 252. |
| cedar-tops | coffin-tap | *P.L.*, VII, 424. | *MD*, I, 294. |
| sea-idol | sea-peasant | *S.A.*, 1. 13. | *MD*, I, 302. |
| chamber-ambushes | cavern-pagoda | *S.A.*, 1. 1112. | *MD*, I, 331. |
| sky-robes | ice-isles | *Comus*, 1. 83. | *MD*, I, 333. |
| lubbar-fiend | sailor-savage | "L'Allegro," 1. 110. | *MD*, I, 343. |
| night-hag | air-sharks | *P.L.*, II, 662. | *MD*, II, 34. |
| Work-master | whale-commanders | *P.L.*, III, 696. | *MD*, II, 39. |
| knee-tribute | child-magician | *P.L.*, V, 782. | *MD*, II, 83. |

| | | | |
|---|---|---|---|
| league-breaker | gold-beater | *S.A.*, 1. 1184. | *MD*, II, 168. |
| heart-grief | heart-woes | *S.A.*, 1. 1339. | *MD*, II, 230. |
| sword-law | stern-wreck | *P.L.*, XI, 672. | *MD*, II, 337. |
| night-wanderer | monk-giver | *P.L.*, IX, 640. | *POB*, XIII, 230. |

## NOUN PLUS PARTICIPLE

| | | | |
|---|---|---|---|
| coral-paven | coral-hung | *Comus*, 1. 886. | *M*, I, 1. |
| self-condemning | self-condemning | *P.L.*, IX, 1188. | *MD*, I, 51. |
| Jove-born | blunder-born | *Comus*, 1. 676. | *MD*, I, 137. |
| joint-racking | wing-folding | *P.L.*, XI, 488. | *MD*, I, 237. |
| ivy-crowned | snow-howdahed | "L'Allegro," 1. 16. | *MD*, I, 242. |
| eagle-winged | hearse-plumed | *P.L.*, VI, 763. | *MD*, I, 279. |
| straw-built | star-belled | *P.L.*, I, 773. | *MD*, II, 166. |
| Heaven-warring | error-abounding | *P.L.*, II, 424. | *MD*, II, 292. |
| heaven-banish'd | god-bullied | *P.L.*, X, 437. | *MD*, II, 366. |
| star-ypointing | Pole-pointed | "Shakespeare," 1. 4. | *MD*, II, 366. |
| planet-struck | winter-overtaken | *P.L.*, X, 413. | *P*, p. 412. |
| wedlock-bound | usage-hardened | *P.L.*, X, 905. | *POB*, XIII, 249. |
| wisdom-giving | party-giving | *P.L.*, IX, 679. | *JR*, XIII, 258. |

## COMPOUNDS WITH "ALL"

| | | | |
|---|---|---|---|
| all-powerful | All-Plastic | *P.L.*, II, 851. | *M*, I, 267. |
| all-seeing | all-seeing | *P.L.*, X, 6. | *MD*, I, 356. |
| all-judging | all-grasping | "Lycidas," 1. 82. | *MD*, II, 124. |
| all-bounteous | all-receptive | *P.L.*, V, 640. | *MD*, II, 256. |
| all-worshipt | all-contributed | *Comus*, 1. 719. | *MD*, II, 256. |
| all-ruling | all-grasping | *P.L.*, I, 212. | *MD*, II, 308. |
| all-conquering | all-destroying | *P.L.*, X, 591. | *MD*, II, 366. |
| all-bearing | all-applauding | *P.L.*, V, 338. | *HF*, XIII, 221. |
| all-cheering | all-fusing | *P.L.*, III, 581. | *CM*, p. 9. |

There is also an unusually large number of compounds with *all* in *Pierre*.

## SUPERLATIVES

| | | | |
|---|---|---|---|
| maturest | arrantest | *P.L.*, II, 115. | *MD*, I, 18. |
| virtuousest | monstrousest | *P.L.*, VIII, 550. | *MD*, I, 89. |
| powerfullest | wonderfullest | *P.L.*, VI, 425. | *MD*, I, 132. |
| prowest | selectest | *P.R.*, III, 342. | *MD*, I, 144. |
| famousest | intensest | *S.A.*, 1. 982. | *MD*, I, 280. |
| constantest | recentest | *S.A.*, 1. 848. | *MD*, II, 252. |
| exquisitest | etherealest | *P.R.*, II, 346. | *P*, p. 48. |
| discreetest | abstractest | *P.L.*, VIII, 550. | *P*, p. 93. |
| fleshliest | sacredest | *P.R.*, II, 152. | *CM*, p. 230. |

## COMPOUNDS OF "UN-"

| | | | |
|---|---|---|---|
| unvoyageable | unsplinterable | *P.L.*, X, 366. | *MD*, I, xii. |
| unsearchable | ungraspable | *P.L.*, VIII, 10. | *MD*, I, 4. |
| unfear'd | unfearing | *P.L.*, IX, 187. | *MD*, I, 145. |
| unappeasable | unappeasedly | *S.A.*, 1. 963. | *MD*, I, 252. |
| unfum'd | uninterpenetratingly | *P.L.*, V, 349. | *MD*, II, 239. |
| unbottom'd | uncontinented | *P.L.*, II, 405. | *MD*, II, 247. |
| unwithdrawing | unmisgiving | *Comus*, 1. 711. | *MD*, II, 314. |
| untractable | untrackably | *P.L.*, X, 476. | *MD*, II, 322. |
| unbenighted | undistrusted | *P.L.*, X, 682. | *P*, p. 89. |
| unhide-bound | unrunagate | *P.L.*, X, 601. | *P*, p. 480. |
| unattending | unresounding | *Comus*, 1. 272. | *P*, p. 482. |
| unconniving | unparticipating | *P.R.*, I, 363. | *CM*, p. 100. |
| undelighted | undelight | *P.L.*, IV, 286. | *Ppo*, XVI, 303. |

## ADJECTIVES IN "-EAN" OR "-IAN" FROM PROPER NOUNS

| | | | |
|---|---|---|---|
| Cerberean | Hyperborean | *P.L.*, II, 655. | *MD*, I, 14. |
| Ausonian | Alleghanian | *P.L.*, I, 739. | *MD*, I, 18. |
| Pygmean | Feegeeans | *P.L.*, I, 780. | *MD*, I, 39. |
| Atlantean | Pannangians | *P.L.*, II, 306. | *MD*, I, 39. |
| Bactrian | Brighggians | *P.L.*, X, 433. | *MD*, I, 39. |
| Tartarean | Tartarian | *P.L.*, II, 69. | *MD*, I, 173. |
| Titanian | Hogarthian | *P.L.*, I, 198. | *MD*, I, 332. |
| Nyseian | Magian | *P.L.*, IV, 275. | *MD*, II, 252. |
| Cathaian | Ephesian | *P.L.*, X, 293, etc. | *MD*, II, 252. |
| Lethean | Semiramian | *P.L.*, II, 604. | *P*, p. 125. |
| Circean | Limeean | *P.L.*, IX, 522. | *P*, p. 210. |
| Sabæan | Hadean | *P.L.*, IV, 162. | *C*, II, 178. |

## REPETITIONS

Burning *fitfully*, and casting *fitful* shadows (*MD*, II, 291).
*Equal* to God, and *equally* enjoying (*P.L.*, III, 306).

Nor did such soothing scenes, however *temporary*, fail of at least as *temporary* an effect on Ahab. But if these *secret golden* keys did seem to open in him his own *secret golden* treasuries . . . (*MD*, II, 264).

> He together calls,/ . . . the *regent* Powers,
> Under him *Regent;* tells, as he was taught,
> That the Most High commanding, *now ere night,*
> *Now ere* dim *night* . . .
>
> (*P.L.*, V, 696–700).

125

His mind *was wandering and vague;* his arm *wandered and was vague* (*P*, p. 235).

> *To pray, repent, and* bring *obedience due.*
> *To prayer, repentence, and obedience due* . . .
> (*P.L.*, III, 190–191).

*He dropped the fatal* volume from *his* hand; *he dropped his fated* head upon *his* chest (*P*, p. 235).

> Before them in a *cloud,* and *pillar of fire;*
> By day a *cloud,* by night a *pillar of fire*
> (*P.L.*, XII, 202–203).

What *wonder* remained *soon waned* away; for in a whaler *wonders soon wane* (*MD*, I, 291).

> *He drew* not *nigh* unheard; the Angel bright,
> Ere *he drew nigh,* his radiant visage turn'd
> (*P.L.*, III, 645–646).

*There, then, he sat, holding up* that imbecile candle in the heart of that almighty forlornness. *There, then, he sat,* the sign and symbol of a man without faith, *hope-*lessly *holding up hope* in the midst of despair (*MD*, I, 284).

> Him . . . / . . . thou didst *not doom*
> *So strictly, but much more to pity incline:*
> No sooner did thy dear and only Son
> Perceive thee purpos'd *not* to *doom* frail Man
> *So strictly, but much more to pity inclin'd* . . .
> (*P.L.*, III, 400–405).

## POSTPOSITIONAL ADJECTIVES

See also Brief Paraphrases, the first section of this appendix.


# APPENDIX C

The following table analyzes and summarizes certain types of evidence presented in earlier parts of this study. No passage by Melville has been included in more than one column, and, in the case of material which is probably but not certainly of Miltonic origin, only those passages in which the probability is strong are included (e.g., passages from *Clarel* I, 108 and 152, discussed on p. 83 above, have not been included). The latter criterion has resulted in the exclusion of all influences mentioned only in the notes, and of all material in Appendix B except that in the first section, Brief Paraphrases.

The columns in the table are headed by letters which have the following meanings:

M  Mention of Milton or of one of his titles.
C  Reference to a character unquestionably from Milton.
C*  Allusion to a character probably from Milton.
S  Reference to a scene unquestionably from Milton.
S*  Allusion to a scene probably from Milton.
I*  Use of an idea probably from Milton.
Q  Quotation certainly from Milton.
Q*  Probable quotation (a passage in quotation marks but too short to be certainly identifiable, or a longer group of words like Milton's but not marked by quotation marks).
P  Extended paraphrase of Milton.
E  Brief paraphrase or verbal echo of Milton.

The difficulty of classifying some passages as showing only one kind of influence makes the distribution into types suggestive rather than conclusive.

| | M | C | C* | S | S* | I* | Q | Q* | P | E | Total |
|---|---|---|---|---|---|---|---|---|---|---|---|
| *FWD* | | | | | | | 1 | | | 1 | 2 |
| *T* | | | | 1 | | | 1 | | | | 2 |
| *O* | | | | | | | 1 | | | | 1 |
| 1847[n] | | | | | | | 1 | | | | 1 |
| *M* | 3 | | 2 | | | 3 | 1 | | 3 | 4 | 16 |
| 1849 | 1 | 1 | 1 | | | | | | | | 3 |
| *R* | 1 | 1 | | 1 | | | 1 | 1 | 1 | 2 | 8 |
| *WJ* | | 1 | 2 | | 1 | | 2 | | | 2 | 8 |
| *J* | | | | | | | 2 | | | | 2 |
| 1850 | 1 | | | | | 1 | | | | 2 | 4 |
| *MD* | | | 5 | | 1 | | 2 | | | 8 | 16 |
| *P* | 1 | | 1 | | | | | | | 4 | 6 |
| *CADD* | | | | | 1 | | | | | 1 | 2 |
| *E* | | | | 1 | 1 | | 1 | | | 2 | 5 |
| *TT* | | | | | | | 1 | | | | 1 |
| *IP* | 1 | | | | | | | | | | 1 |
| *POB* | | | | | | | | | 1 | | 1 |
| *IAMC* | | | | | | | | | 1 | | 1 |
| *Pi* | | | 1 | | | | | | | | 1 |
| *CM* | | 1 | 2 | | 2 | 1 | | | | 2 | 8 |
| *JUS* | | | | 1 | 1 | 1 | | | | | 3 |
| 1857 | 1 | | | | | | | | | | 1 |
| 1858 | 2 | | | | | | | 1 | | | 3 |
| 1860 | 1 | | | | | | 1 | | | | 2 |
| *BP* | | | 4 | | 1 | | | | 2 | 6 | 13 |
| 1875 | | | 1 | | | | | | | | 1 |
| *C* | | 1 | 2 | | 1 | | | | 1 | 8 | 13 |
| *Tim* | | | | | 1 | | | | | 3 | 4 |
| *Ppo* | | | 1 | | | | | | | 1 | 2 |
| *Ppr* | | 1 | | | | | | | | 1 | 2 |
| *BB* | | | | | | | 1 | | | | 1 |
| Total sure: | 12 | 6 | — | 3 | — | — | 13 | — | — | — | 34 |
| probable: | — | — | 22 | — | 11 | 4 | | 7 | 9 | 47 | 100 |
| From *P.L.*: | 3 | 6 | 22 | 3 | 10 | 3 | 10 | 5 | 7 | 35 | 104 |
| other works: | 9 | — | — | — | 1 | 1 | 3 | 2 | 2 | 12 | 30 |

[n]The dates in the left-hand column are the years of letters, uncollected writings, and notes in association volumes in which evidence of Milton's influence appears. All works are arranged chronologically for probable date of final revision.

# NOTES

*"All subjects are inexhaustible."*
—Mardi, *II, 106.*

## Chapter One
[Pages 1–17]

1. Raymond Dexter Havens, *The Influence of Milton on English Poetry* (Cambridge, Mass., 1922), p. [vii].

2. *Mardi*, II, 277.

3. F. O. Matthiessen, *American Renaissance* (N.Y., 1941), pp. 101–102.

4. See, for example, Charles Roberts Anderson, *Melville in the South Seas* (N.Y., 1939); Melville, *Journal up the Straits*, ed. Raymond M. Weaver (N.Y., 1935); and Henry F. Pommer, "Herman Melville and the Wake of the *Essex*," *Am. Lit.*, XX (November, 1948), 290–304.

5. See, for example, Keith Huntress, "Melville's Use of a Source for *White-Jacket*," *Am. Lit.*, XVII (March, 1945), 66–74; and Anderson, *Melville in the South Seas, passim.*

6. See the Introduction to *Melville, Billy Budd*, ed. F. Barron Freeman (Cambridge, [1948]), and below.

7. *Mardi*, I, 16. The material of this and of the next paragraph is treated at much greater length in Henry F. Pommer, *Milton's Influence on Herman Melville* (unpublished dissertation in the Yale University Library, 1946), pp. 8–24.

8. *Mardi*, I, 230.

9. *Billy Budd*, XIII, 29.

10. Oscar Wegelin, "Herman Melville as I Recall Him," *Colophon*, n.s.I (Summer, 1935), 21–24; p. 23.

11. See Appendix A.

12. *Pierre*, pp. 394–395; cf. p. 127.

13. William Braswell, "Melville's Use of Seneca," *Am. Lit.*, XII (March, 1940), 98–104.

14. See, for example, Matthiessen's study of the Shakespearean element in *Moby-Dick* in *American Renaissance*, pp. 412–417 and 423–435.

15. *Mardi*, I, 13; II, 54, 90, and 323–324; italics in original. Cf. the same idea in *Redburn* (p. 190): "In all our erections, however imposing, we but form quar-

ries and supply ignoble materials for the grander domes of posterity." It is interesting that in his copy of *Fingal*, acquired the year before *Mardi*, Melville underlined and checked this sentence: "The actions of other times are in my soul: my memory beams on the days that are past." (*Fingal*, 2d ed., translated by James Macpherson [London, 1762], p. 261; Melville's copy is in the Princeton University Library.) See also Matthiessen, *American Renaissance*, pp. 629–630.

16.  H.M. to E.A.D., March 3, 1849 (*Herman Melville: Representative Selections*, ed. Willard Thorp [N.Y., 1938], p. 371).

17.  *Pierre*, p. 191.

18.  *Redburn*, pp. 145–146; italics in original.

19.  *Billy Budd*, XIII, 93.

20.  See notes 5 and 13 above.

21.  The material of this paragraph is presented with much greater detail in Pommer, *Milton's Influence on Herman Melville*, pp. 26–36.

22.  William C. Macready, "Poetry and Its Influence on Popular Education," *The Literary World*, XI (July 10, 1852), 27–30; p. 30.

23.  Melville's copy of *The English Reader* is now in the Gansevoort-Lansing Collection of the N.Y.P.L. The title-page is missing, but the title is stamped on the spine. I have determined the editorship of the volume by comparing the association copy with complete copies of Murray's once very popular work. I have not yet found a perfectly matching edition, but the following has only a few minor variations from Melville's: *The English Reader*, ed. Lindley Murray (N.Y., stereotyped by B. & J. Collins, printed and sold by Collins and Co., [1802?]). The material in my text is based on pp. [iii], ix, xvi, 155, 217, 239–240, and 207–209 of the Melville copy.

24.  *The London Carcanet*, from the Second London Edition (N.Y., 1831), pp. 31, 38, 51, 84, and 32. The volume is owned by Mr. Alexander Orr Vietor.

25.  William Braswell, *Melville's Religious Thought* (Durham, 1943), pp. 4–8.

26.  Hester Mulso Chapone, *Letters on the Improvement of the Mind* (Boston, 1809), pp. 141, 142; italics in original. The volume is now in the possession of Mrs. Eleanor Melville Metcalf.

27.  "Remarks on the Character and Writings of John Milton," *The Works of William E. Channing*, Eighth Complete Edition (Boston, 1848), 6 vols., I, 3–68; pp. 4, 3, 39–40. The volumes are the property of Mrs. Frances T. Osborne and are on deposit in the N.Y.P.L.

28.  Matthiessen, *American Renaissance*, p. 103.

29.  Elizabeth Shaw Melville to E.A.D., June 23, 1860 (Meade Minnigerode, *Some Personal Letters of Herman Melville and a Bibliography* (N.Y., 1922), p. 87.

30.  J. B. Auld to George L. Duyckinck, September, 1847 (Luther Stearns Mansfield, *Herman Melville: Author and New Yorker, 1844–1851* [unpublished dissertation in the University of Chicago Library, 1936], pp. 62–66 and 27). The quotation is from *Paradise Lost*, VII, 323.

31.  The periodicals were *Yankee Doodle* and *The Literary World*. For material

which they contained on Milton, see *Yankee Doodle*, II (August 28, 1847), 208; *The Literary World*, II (September 25, 1847), 182–183; III (July 22, 1848), 481–483; IV (April 21, 1849), 350–351; VII (December 28, 1850), 525; IX (August 2, 1851), 86–87; XI (July 10, 1852), 30; XII (April 2, 1853), 269; XIII (September 10 and November 5, 1853), 110 and 232. For Melville's connections with the periodicals and their editors, see Luther Stearns Mansfield, "Melville's Comic Articles on Zachary Taylor," *Am. Lit.*, IX (January, 1938), 411–418; *Selections*, ed. Thorp, pp. 374, 381–384, 421; Melville, "To Major John Gentian," XIII, 362; Christine H. Hunter, *A Study in Herman Melville's Sketches and Tales* (unpublished M.A. essay in Yale University Library, 1941), p. 17; H.M. to *The Literary World*, February 14, 1852 (unpublished manuscript in the Duyckinck Collection of N.Y.P.L.).

32. "Duyckinck Collection," *Lenox Library Short-Title Lists*, No. 8 (1887), 41 and No. 12 (1890), 66; and catalogue of N.Y.P.L. The two sources do not completely agree as to what volumes were in Duyckinck's library.

33. *Alphabetical and Analytical Catalogue of the New York Society Library* (N.Y., 1850), pp. 299–300.

34. Elizabeth Manning Hawthorne to James T. Fields, December, 1870 (Randall Stewart, "Recollections of Hawthorne by his Sister Elizabeth," *Am. Lit.*, XVI [January, 1945], 316–331, p. 319); Matthiessen, *American Renaissance*, pp. 305–312; Nathaniel Hawthorne, *The American Notebooks*, ed. Randall Stewart (New Haven, 1932), *passim;* Nathaniel Hawthorne, *The English Notebooks*, ed. Randall Stewart (N.Y., 1941), *passim.*

35. See, below, n. 53 of Chapter V, and n. 12 of Chapter III.

36. *White Jacket*, p. 262. Performances of *The Creation* in New York on May 14, 1847, and March 11, 1848, and of *Samson* in New York and Brooklyn on March 25, 1847, and June 7, 1849, are recorded in George C. D. Odell, *Annals of the New York Stage* (N.Y., 1927–1945), 14 vols., V, 315, 405, and 510–511. Other performances of the same oratorios between 1845 and 1850 are noted by Odell, but for dates when Melville was probably or certainly not in New York.

37. Letter to me from Mrs. Eleanor Melville Metcalf, who owns the drawing. My frontispiece was reproduced from John Milton, *Paradise Lost*, ill. John Martin (London, 1833), opp. p. 29. Edwin White's *The Old Age of Milton* must have come to Melville's attention through the American Art-Union, of which Evert Duyckinck was a member of the Committee of Management for 1848, and Allan Melville a member for 1848 (*Transactions of the American Art-Union, for the Year 1848* [N.Y., 1849], pp. [3], 54, 152). Edwin White's *The Old Age of Galileo*, with Milton as a prominent figure, is described in the *Bulletin of the American Art-Union*, No. 3 (May 25, 1848), 6.

38. Raymond M. Weaver, *Herman Melville: Mariner and Mystic* (N.Y., 1921), pp. 304 and 376. Cf. the engravings in the family dining-room in *Redburn*, p. 5, and the description of a negro church in *Moby-Dick*, I, 10.

39. *Journal up the Straits*, p. 149.

40. "Il Penseroso," ll. 31–42. "Hiram Powers," *Dictionary of American Biography*

ed. Allen Johnson and others (N.Y., 1928–1937), 20 vols., XV, 159. The illustration given here is from a photograph in the N.Y.P.L., to which *Il Penseroso* at one time belonged; the statue is now reported lost. In 1871 Powers finished a female nude entitled *Paradise Lost* (*Catalogue of the A. T. Stewart Collection of Paintings, Sculptures*..., Illustrated Edition [N.Y., 1887], pp. 177–178, illustration following p. 164).

41. Henry A. Murray, "Personality and Creative Imagination," *English Institute Annual, 1942* (N.Y., 1943), pp. 139–162; p. 161.

42. Like most western thinkers of the Christian era, Melville was acutely aware of the fall of man in Paradise, and of its theological or symbolic meaning. He would, of course, have been so even if there had never been a Milton in our culture, and therefore it is difficult to assess the influence of *Paradise Lost* on this part of his thinking. For example, should Milton be mentioned in connection with Boynton's remark about *Moby-Dick*, that

> beneath this whaling adventure ... is the story of Eve or of Prometheus, the perennial story of man's struggle for spiritual victory in a world of harassing circumstance and in a world where fate opposes the individual in the form of his own thwarting self

(*Literature and American Life* [Boston, 1936], p. 469)? In discussing Melville's "preoccupation ... with the Fall," Matthiessen raises the possibility of his having mentioned Dryden in a marginal comment because of *The State of Innocence, and Fall of Man* (*American Renaissance*, p. 502). I know of no evidence that Melville ever read that dramatic version of *Paradise Lost*. At the same time Matthiessen points out the interesting fact that in his copy of Schopenhauer's *Studies in Pessimism*, tr. T. Bailey Saunders (London, 1891; now in the Houghton Library of Harvard University) Melville scored these sentences:

> The sole thing that reconciles me to the Old Testament is the story of the Fall. In my eyes, it is the only metaphysical truth in that book, even though it appears in the form of an allegory.

*Matthiessen*

43. *Pierre*, p. 412.

44. Merton M. Sealts, *Herman Melville's Reading in Ancient Philosophy* (unpublished dissertation in Yale University Library, 1942), pp. 110–111.

45. *P.L.*, VIII, 84.

46. *Mardi*, II, 161.

47. *P.L.*, VIII, 167–168. Tyrus Hillway has pointed out ("Taji's Quest for Certainty," *Am. Lit.*, XVIII [March, 1946], 27–34; p. 32) a parallel between the thought of the lines just quoted, and Babbalanja's statement that "beyond one obvious mark, all human lore is vain." (*Mardi*, II, 371.) Nathalia Wright has observed of the next chapter ("Babbalanja Relates to them a Vision," *Ibid.*, II, 373–379) that "the landscape is Miltonic or Dantesque." (*Melville's Use of the Bible* [Durham, 1949], p. 160.) It does remind us of Raphael's discourse with Adam in Book VIII, and we can find Miltonic diction, rhythm, similes, and grammar at work in Melville's prose.

It is perhaps merely a curious fact that as Raphael presented two contesting systems of astronomy without supporting either (*P.L.*, VIII, 66–178), just so

Babbalanja presents impartially two systems of geology (*Mardi*, II, 111–113).

48. *Journals of Ralph Waldo Emerson*, ed. Edward Waldo Emerson and Waldo Emerson Forbes (Boston, 1909–1914) 10 vols., V, 256. Cf. *The Complete Works of Ralph Waldo Emerson*, ed. Edward Waldo Emerson, Centenary Edition (Boston, 1903–1904), 12 vols.; X, 99–100.

49. *Billy Budd*, XIII, 29. Further evidence on this point will be found in the first section of Chapter VII.

50. *The Poetical Works of Thomas Chatterton*, . . . (Cambridge, 1842), 2 vols., II, 446. The volumes are in the Berg Collection of the N.Y.P.L. Opposite the title page of Volume I, Melville wrote: "Herman Melville London Dec: 19. 1849. Bought at a dirty stall there, and got it bound near by." In his *Journal of a Visit to London and the Continent, 1849–1850* (ed. Eleanor Melville Metcalf [Cambridge, 1948]), Melville noted the purchase of the volumes in the entry for December 18; they were probably delivered from the binder on the next day. Both volumes were given by Melville to his brother-in-law, John C. Hoadley, on January 6, 1854, as another ms. note opposite the title page of Volume I indicates.

51. *Moby-Dick*, I, 133; cf. I, 73: "that turnpike earth!"

52. *P.L.*, VII, 25–26.

53. *Selections*, ed. Thorp, p. xiii.

54. Hawthorne, *English Notebooks*, p. 432.

55. *P.L.*, II, 558–561.

56. Stanley Geist, *Herman Melville: The Tragic Vision and the Heroic Ideal* (Cambridge, 1939), pp. 18, 48, and 64.

57. "Hawthorne and His Mosses," XIII, 129. Cf. "The spirit of his old Puritan ancestors, to whom he refers in the preface [of *The Scarlet Letter*], lives in Nathaniel Hawthorne" (Melville, "Nathaniel Hawthorne," *The Literary World*, VI [March 30, 1850], 323–325; p. 324).

58. "Hawthorne and His Mosses," XIII, 139.

59. William Braswell, "Melville as a Critic of Emerson," *Am. Lit.*, IX (November, 1937), 317–334.

60. William Ellery Sedgwick, *Herman Melville: The Tragedy of Mind* (Cambridge, 1944), pp. 27–28.

61. Paul Elmer More, "The Theme of *Paradise Lost*" *Shelburne Essays*, Fourth Series (N.Y., and London, 1907), pp. 239–253; pp. 243–244.

62. Douglas Bush, *Paradise Lost in Our Time* (Ithaca, N.Y., 1945), p. 80.

63. *Moby-Dick*, I, 183. Cf. *Ibid.*, I, 91–92, 99, 144; *Redburn*, p. 356; *Billy Budd*, XIII, 49–50.

64. *P.L.*, IX, 36.

65. *Moby-Dick*, I, 183, 133; II, 220.

66. *Pierre*, p. 394.

67. "Self-Reliance," *The Complete Works of Ralph Waldo Emerson*, II, 43–90; p. 46.

# Chapter Two

[Pages 18–28]

1. Braswell, *Melville's Religious Thought*, pp. 13 and 130 (italics in original).

2. A. S. W. Rosenbach, *An Introduction to Herman Melville's Moby-Dick* (N.Y., 1924), p. 6.

3. Walter Weber, *Herman Melville, eine stilistische Untersuchung* (Basel, 1937), p. 9. Here and in the later quotations from Weber, the translations are ones which I have made with the kind assistance of Professor Lydia Baer of Swarthmore College.

4. Nathalia Wright, "Biblical Allusion in Melville's Prose," *Am. Lit.*, XII (May, 1940), 185–199; p. 198.

5. *Omoo*, p. 38; *Clarel*, II, 90.

6. Melville's mention of Milton's presence in Italy is discussed on p. 110.

7. *Redburn*, p. 244. The beggar's chant has a suggestive similarity to *S.A.*, 11. 80 and 86–87:

> *O dark, dark, dark . . .*
> *The sun to me is dark,*
> *And silent as the moon.*

8. *Mardi*, II, 54 and 320. Begging, groping, blindness, and the sun link the second of these quotations with that quoted immediately above from *Redburn*. Further descriptions of the blind poet, Vavona, his loneliness and self-esteem, may be based on Milton's life (*Mardi*, II, 86, 89, and 320).

9. *P.L.*, III, 32–36.

10. *Mardi*, II, 241.

11. K. H. Sundermann suggests (*Herman Melvilles Gedankengut* [Berlin, 1937], p. 60 and p. 201, n. 27) a comparison between the following passages:

> *I shudder at idea of ancient Egyptians. It was in these pyramids that was conceived the idea of Jehovah. Terrible mixture of the cunning and awful. Moses learned in all the lore of the Egyptians. The idea of Jehovah born here.* [Journal up the Straits, *p. 58.*]
>
> *The Israelites learnt a great deal of wickedness in Egypt.* [A Defense of the People of England, *II, 46.*]

In other passages Milton expresses similar disdain of the Egyptians who held the Israelites in bondage, but none seems to me significantly close to the passage in Melville's journal.

12. *Pierre*, p. 233.

13. *Areopagitica*, I, 174 and 168. The following passage from *White Jacket* (p. 287) has its own resemblances to ideas in *Areopagitica*:

> *When Virtue rules by compulsion, and domineers over Vice as a slave, then Virtue, though her mandates be outwardly observed, bears little interior sway.*

14. Melville, "A Thought on Book-Binding," *The Literary World*, VI (March 16, 1850), 276–277.

15.  *Clarel*, I, 307.

16.  *White Jacket*, p. 4.

17.  *Of Education*, I, 160. Cf. *Redburn*, p. 359: "At last Harry sat among them like *Orpheus* among the *charmed* leopards and tigers."

18.  "Lycidas," ll. 58–59.

19.  John Livingston Lowes, *The Road to Xanadu* (Boston, 1927), pp. 56–63.

20.  "Fragments from a Writing-Desk," XIII, 388; "L'Allegro," l. 136.

21.  "L'Allegro," ll. 25–28. See also p. 149, n. 36, below.

22.  Melville, Review of *Etchings of a Whaling Cruise* and *Sailors' Life and Sailors' Yarns*, *The Literary World*, I (March 6, 1847), 105–106; p. 106.

23.  "The Two Temples," XIII, 179.

24.  "The Encantadas," X, 238–239. In Schopenhauer's *Wisdom of Life* Melville checked and underlined the sentence "The lust for fame is the last that a wise man shakes off" (*Billy Budd*, ed. Freeman, p. 25).

25.  "Lycidas," ll. 70–71.

26.  *Moby-Dick*, I, 78 and 86. Cf. *Mardi*, II, 211; "Thou art *most musical*, sweet Yoomy."

27.  "Il Penseroso," l. 62.

28.  *American Renaissance*, p. 494.

29.  "A Requiem," *Battle-Pieces*, XVI, 128. The last line quoted here from Melville is reminiscent of another Miltonic passage which, as we have seen, Melville knew well—part of the "Invocation to the Sun":

> *Thee I* revisit *safe,*
> *And feel thy sovran vital lamp; but thou*
> Revisit'st *not these eyes.*
> [P.L., *III, 21–23.*]

30.  "Lycidas," ll. 62–63 and 154–160. It is perhaps worth noting that the theme of immortality in "Lycidas" as well as the phrasing of l. 157 are anticipative of the final couplet of *Clarel* (II, 298):

> *Emerge thou mayst from the last whelming sea,*
> *And prove that death but routs life into victory.*

31.  H. M. to George L. Duyckinck, November 6, 1858 (unpublished manuscript in the Duyckinck Collection of N.Y.P.L.).

32.  *Clarel*, I, 237. Cf. "On the Morning of Christ's Nativity," ll. 178 and 200, and *P.L.*, I, 439. With the exile of the pagan deities in Milton's poem, compare *Clarel*, II, 187 (italics in original):

> *When rule and era passed away*
> *With old Sylvanus (stories say),*
> *The oracles adrift were hurled,*
> *And ocean moaned about the world,*
> *And wandering voices without name*

> *At sea to sailors did proclaim,*
> Pan, Pan is dead!

33. "Paradise of Bachelors," XIII, 228.

34. "Il Penseroso," 11. 49–50. Lines 83–84 have a rhythm like Melville's. The following quotation from *Mardi* (I, 310) also captures some of the rhythm and a phrase from "Il Penseroso":

> . . . twilight groves, *and dreamy meads; hither gliding, thither fading, end or purpose none.*

Cf. "To arched walks of *twilight groves*" ("Il Penseroso," 1. 133).

35. For less important verbal echoes of the minor poems, of *P.R.*, and of *Comus*, see Appendix B.

# Chapter Three
### [Pages 29–49]

1. Lewis Mumford, *Herman Melville* (N.Y., 1929), p. 182.

2. Jean Simon, *Herman Melville, Marin, Métaphysicien et Poète* (Paris, 1939), p. 577.

3. *Typee*, p. 296.

4. *The Faerie Queene*, I, ix, 15, 5. In Pope's "no face divine contentment wears," ("Eloisa to Abelard," 1. 147) *divine* appears to modify *contentment* rather than *face*. I have failed to find the expression in concordances of the poetry of Burns, Chaucer, Coleridge, Collins, Cowper, Donne, Emerson, Goldsmith, Gray, Herrick, Keats, Poe, Shakespeare, Shelley, Tennyson, Wordsworth, and Wyatt. Of course the phrase may exist in any number of minor poets whom Melville may have read.

5. *P.L.*, III, 44. In lines 140–141 of the same Book appears

> *and in his face*
> *Divine compassion visibly appear'd,*

where *Divine* might possibly be construed as modifying *face*. Sara Jane Lippincott used the former phrase from *P.L.* when she parodied *Typee* in 1847: "in the form of 'the *human face divine*'" (Willard Thorp, "'Grace Greenwood' Parodies *Typee*," *Am. Lit.*, IX [January, 1938], 455–457; p. 457).

6. Eclogues, i, 24. *P.L.*, II, 921–922. Milton has slightly different versions of the clause in *P.L.*, VI, 310–311; X, 306; and *P.R.*, IV, 563–564.

7. *Omoo*, p. 40. Did Melville know Milton's Latin poems on Guy Fawkes' Day?

8. *P.L.*, I, 549–551; *Redburn*, p. 220.

9. *P.L.*, I, 711–712. For Melville's quoting the first words of 1. 711, see p. 109.

10. *Redburn*, p. 122; *P.L.*, II, 404–407.

11. "Hawthorne and His Mosses," XIII, 130.

12. *P.L.*, I, 200–202 and VII, 412–416; *The Whale* (London, 1851). Hollywood borrowed from the first of these passages to give the film version of *Moby-Dick* its

title, *The Sea Beast* (Melville, *Moby-Dick or The White Whale: Photoplay Title "The Sea Beast"* [N.Y., (1925)]).

Mansfield has stated (*Melville*, p. 218) that approximately a dozen of the "Extracts" in *Moby-Dick* were taken from Henry T. Cheever's *The Whale and his Captors* (N.Y., 1850), including these two from *Paradise Lost.* A careful comparison of the readings in Cheever and in the first edition of *Moby-Dick* (N.Y., 1851) shows such variations in wording, spelling, and punctuation that the precise text from which Melville quoted remains in doubt.

13.  *Confidence-Man*, p. 27; *P.L.*, II, 14–17.

14.  *Journal up the Straits*, p. 17; *P.L.*, I, 746.

15.  From a review of Melville's lecture, "Statuary in Rome," Cincinnati *Daily Gazette* (February 3, 1858): reprinted in The Editors, "Melville and his Public: 1858," *American Notes and Queries*, II (August, 1942), 67–71; p. 69. The statue to which Melville referred in the lecture is probably the one pictured in the text, *La caduta degli angeli ribelli* by Agostino Fasolato. This statue is in Padua, not Rome. I have failed to locate any statue in Rome which fits the description, whereas Fasolato's work fits both the description above and an entry in *Journal up the Straits* (Padua, April 1, 1857; p. 152): "To the . . . [illegible] palace to see the 'Satan & his host.' Fine attitude of Satan Intricate as heap of vermicelli." Professor Sergio Bettini, Director of the Civic Museum in Padua, put me greatly in his debt by locating the statue in the Palazzo Papafava. Professor Bettini has written to me that it is quite understandable that Melville might have praised the marble group after a brief study of it, delighting in its subject rather than analyzing its artistic value. Professor Bettini adds that Melville probably confused one of the angels with Satan, who is really at the bottom, in the form of an infernal monster.

16.  *P.L.*, I, 107–108. My reason for saying that it was probably Melville and not his reviewer who quoted Milton is that the sentence just quoted from the review immediately follows a specific mention of Milton considered on p. 110.

17.  *P.L.*, I, 711. Melville's copy of *The Iliads of Homer*, tr. George Chapman (London, 1857), 2 vols., is in the Houghton Library. The quotation from *P.L.* is on I, 14, and notes in the front of the volume in Melville's hand read "H. Melville from George Duyckinck Pittsfield Nov. 1858" and "C[ape]. H[orn]. 2." For Melville's second rounding of Cape Horn see "Journal of Melville's Voyage in a Clipper Ship," *New England Quarterly*, II (January, 1929), 120–125.

18.  *Billy Budd*, XIII, 48; *P.L.*, IV, 115. A slightly different setting for the quotation appears in *Billy Budd*, ed. Freeman, p. 190, n. 1. Melville's version gives *Pale* an adjectival function instead of its original substantive one. Of the numerous editions of *Paradise Lost* published before 1850 which I have examined, four omit the comma after *Pale*, lending some authority to Melville's punctuation. For the significance of Melville's punctuation, see p. 88.

19.  *P.L.*, IV, 156–166. "Gentle gales" appears in the preceding chapter in a quotation from "Fragments from a Writing-Desk."

20.  *Mardi*, II, 228.

21. *White Jacket*, p. 69.

22. *Clarel*, II, 75 and 225; note the Miltonism, "freshening redolence divine." Cf. *Redburn*, p. 386 ("to our salted lungs the land breeze was spiced with aromas") and *Moby-Dick*, I, 41 ("Salem, where they tell me the young girls breathe such musk, their sailor sweet-hearts *smell* them miles off *shore*, as though they were drawing nigh the *odorous* Moluccas instead of the Puritanic sands") and *Ibid.*, II, 126.

23. *Journal 1849*, October 13, 1849; *P.L.*, II, 560. Matthiessen concurs in my wording of the passage, and adds, "In quoting this line from *Paradise Lost*, Melville was doubtless aware that the next line added: 'And found no end, in wandering mazes lost.' " (*American Renaissance*, p. 455.) This passage from *P.L.* suggests some of the lunatics whom Isabel described in *Pierre* (p. 170).

24. *Journal 1849*, page in the manuscript following entry for January 30, 1850. Weaver prints this quotation as part of the 1856 journal and states that it "occupies a page to itself." (*Journal up the Straits*, p. 1.) It does not occupy a page by itself, although it is written on the page which separates the last dated entry of the earlier trip from the first dated entry of the later trip, the one to the Holy Lands.

25. *Pierre*, p. 254. Cf. the discussion of foreknowledge, *Ibid.*, p. 400.

26. *P.L.*, II, 558–560; "The Age of the Antonines," *Timoleon*, XVI, 273–274.

27. *Colossians*, i, 16.

28. *Mardi*, I, 14.

29. *P.L.*, III, 320; V, 601, 772, and 840; X, 460 and 86–87.

30. H.M. to E.A.D., August 16, 1850. Thorp concurs in my reading of the manuscript (*Selections*, p. 381).

31. "The Encantadas," X, 196–197.

32. *P.L.*, XII, 646–647.

33. *Ibid.*, VIII, 332–333; IX, 11. *World* and *woe* are also linked in I, 3; X, 984.

34. *Moby-Dick*, I, 58 and 54. Cf. "world of woes," ("Cock-A-Doodle-Doo!" XIII, 158), p. 76 below.

35. *P.L.*, III, 1–6; "In the Desert," *Timoleon*, XVI, 292.

36. Homer, *Iliads*, II, 208.

37. *P.L.*, VII, 247; XI, 731; III, 361. Did the rhyme of "spher'd" and "smear'd" link the first two phrases in Melville's mind?

38. Weaver, *Melville*, p. 285. Cf. n. 23 above.

39. Minnigerode, *Personal Letters of Melville*, p. 68. Cf. n. 30 above. Somerset Maugham used his knowledge of Milton's vocabulary in his criticism of *Moby-Dick*: "Sometimes [in reading *Moby-Dick*] one is pulled up by such a tautology as 'hasty precipitancy' only to discover with some awe that Milton wrote: 'Thither they hasted with glad precipitance.' . . . When [Melville] . . . speaks of 'redundant hair,' it may occur to you that hair may be redundant on a maiden's lip, but hardly on a young man's head; but if you look it up in the dictionary you will find that the second sense of redundant is copious, and Milton (Milton again!) wrote of 'redundant locks.' . . . [Melville's] style . . . does indeed often recall the majestic phrase of Sir

Thomas Browne and the stately period of Milton." (Somerset Maugham, "Moby Dick," *The Atlantic*, CLXXXI [June, 1948], 98–104; p. 103.)

40.  *Redburn*, pp. 83–84.

41.  Additional instances for some points of my analysis can be found in Weber's strangely mechanical examination of Melville's prose, and in such limited studies as James Mark Purcell, "Melville's Contribution to English," *Publications of the Modern Language Association*, LVI (September, 1941), 797–808. For Milton, see, for example, David Masson, "Syntax and Idiom," *The Poetical Works of John Milton* (London, 1882), 3 vols., III, 186–206; Havens, *Influence of Milton*, pp. 80–85; James Holly Hanford, *A Milton Handbook*, Third Edition (N.Y., 1941), pp. 293–311 and Bibliography.

42.  *Redburn*, pp. 275 and p. 6; italics in original.

43.  Joseph Addison, *Criticism of Milton's Paradise Lost, From 'The Spectator,'* ed. Edward Arber (London, 1868), pp. 34, 36; *Spectator* No. CCLXXXV.

44.  See Appendix B.

45.  Havens notes "words in general use but employed by Milton in senses obsolete in the eighteenth century. To such words he usually gives the meanings they had in Latin or Anglo Saxon." (*Influence of Milton*, pp. 83–84.) Weber says, "The situation is the same with many loan-words, Latinisms, Grecisms, scientific and technical endings and in many cases with historical, geographical, ethnological singularities also. Even though certain conclusions can rarely be derived from definite points of contact, nevertheless a great deal betrays itself as belonging to the world of Rabelais, Milton, Browne, and Carlyle." (*Stilistische Untersuchung*, p. 56.)

46.  *Moby-Dick*, II, 348; cf. II, 41; *Mardi*, I, 247; II, 227; and *White Jacket*, p. 76. *P.L.*, V, 890.

47.  *Ibid.*, II, 108; cf. "Fragments of a Lost Gnostic Poem," *Timoleon*, XVI, 272. *P.L.*, I, 623–624; etc.

48.  "The Lake," Posthumous Poetry, XVI, 431; *P.L.*, VII, 281–282.

49.  *Mardi*, II, 373; *P.L.*, IV, 800–804.

50.  *Moby-Dick*, I, 291; *P.L.*, I, 2.

51.  *Clarel*, I, 127; *P.L.*, II, 51.

52.  *Moby-Dick*, I, 324; cf. "The Bell-Tower," X, 266; *Mardi*, II, 243. *P.L.*, III, 21–22.

53.  See Appendix B.

54.  Evidence of Melville's knowledge of Latin exists throughout his works, and would provide the material for a scholarly article.

55.  Havens, *Influence of Milton*, pp. 80, 84.

56.  *Mardi*, II, 377. For further analysis of Melville's compounding of words see Weber, *Stilistische Untersuchung*, pp. 44–48.

57.  H. L. Mencken, *The American Language*, Fourth Edition (N.Y., 1937), *passim*. Melville is closest to a boisterously American use of compounds in *Mardi*, I, 279.

58. See Appendix B. "These random examples [of compound epithets and metaphor in *Billy Budd*] . . . are not mere lively 'asides' to the narrative but integral parts of the tale. The use of epithet and metaphor was a basic device in Melville's creative methods." (*Billy Budd*, ed. Freeman, p. 112.)

59. Havens, *Influence of Milton*, p. 82.

60. *Moby-Dick*, II, 166; *P.L.*, IV, 536.

61. *Clarel*, I, 309; *P.L.*, III, 533–534. In the latter instance, as well as in *P.L.*, VII, 504, Milton retains some of the Latin sense of "crowded" which Melville has lost.

62. Havens, *Influence of Milton*, p. 82.

63. *Redburn*, p. 122; *Moby-Dick*, II, 300; *P.R.*, IV, 433–434.

64. *Moby-Dick*, I, 350 and II, 326; *P.L.*, I, 297.

65. *Redburn*, p. 371; *White Jacket*, p. 496; *P.L.*, II, 980. *Profound* may be used as a noun in *P.L.*, II, 438 also.

66. *Moby-Dick*, I, 133; *P.L.*, III, 12.

67. "Man-of-War Hawk," *John Marr*, XVI, 235; *P.L.*, IX, 125.

68. *Mardi*, II, 188; *P.L.*, IV, 556–557.

69. *Moby-Dick*, II, 355; *Mardi*, I, 353; *P.L.*, VI, 440, 646–647.

70. *Mardi*, II, 273 and I, 1, 5; *Moby-Dick*, II, 186; "Encantadas," X, 190.

71. *P.L.*, VII, 324–326; IX, 426; I, 234; VII, 50; VI, 543.

72. See Appendix B.

73. See Appendix B. There is an unusually large number of compounds with *un-* in *Pierre*. It is interesting to speculate on the connection between Milton's and Melville's use of *un-*, and a phenomenon noted by Sir William A. Craigie:

> *While I was reading some proofs of the* Oxford English Dictionary[,] *I observed that in the case of two or three words beginning with the prefix* un- *the older quotations (from the seventeenth century) were from English sources, while the later (of the eighteenth century) were all American. . . . It seemed probable that the use of the words had continued later in this country than at home.* ["*The Historical Dictionary of American English*," English Journal, *XV (January, 1926), 13–23; p. 14.*]

74. Weber might add this characteristic (*Stilistische Untersuchung*, pp. 53–54):

> *A whole host of person and place names, particularly in* Mardi, *are to be considered as oddities of sound. They probably owe their origin to the same artistic impulse which has already revealed itself in vocabulary as frank joy in what is unusual, archaistic, or exotic. This group of coinages disappears again in the later works except for rare traces. In any case it must be traced back to Milton, Rabelais, and possibly also to Swift's influence.*

75. Havens, *Influence of Milton*, p. 85. For examples of such adjectives, see Appendix B.

76. *Mardi*, I, 31. Italics in original.

77. *Selections*, ed. Thorp, pp. xiv, cxxx.

78.  *Pierre*, p. 341; *Moby-Dick*, I, 307.

79.  H.M. to E.A.D., December 12, 1850 (*Selections*, ed. Thorp, p. 383).

80.  *Moby-Dick*, II, 234.

81.  Havens mentions "the intentional repetition of a word or a phrase" as a characteristic "which must have pleased Milton's ear (since it occurs frequently in all his poems)" but which is "so common in earlier poetry as to be, in my opinion, of no value in determining influence." (*Influence of Milton*, p. 85.) Weber mentions Milton in his treatment of "Literarische Abhängigkeit" in his section on "Repetition and Variation." (*Stilistische Untersuchung*, p. 115.)

82.  In discussing literary influences on the parallelisms of Melville's prose, Weber says:

> *The spirit of the Renaissance is continued in the Meditations of John Donne, the prose works of Milton (in his poetry parallelism appears only as antithesis), and above all Sir Thomas Browne's philosophical works. . . . According to his own testimony, Melville was deeply influenced by all three, and especially by Browne, whose great effectiveness must be traced to the constant interplay of antithesis and the considered see-saw of paired groups of words.* [Ibid., *pp. 94–95.*]

83.  *Moby-Dick*, II, 250; *P.L.*, IV, 288–289.

84.  See Appendix B.

85.  *Pierre*, p. 423; *P.L.*, IV, 641–656. Cf. "Paradise of Bachelors," XIII, 228: "Sweet are. . . . "

86.  See, for example, *Moby-Dick*, II, 300; *P.L.*, VI, 621–627.

87.  "A second feature of Milton's style which is also to be found in the work of his predecessors is the use of an uninterrupted series of words in the same construction, —participles, adjectives, verbs, substantives, etc. . . . Such series are not frequent in *Paradise Lost*, however, and might be used independently of Milton." (Havens, *Influence of Milton*, p. 85.) Among other influences, "[after the Elizabethan period] Milton gave cumulation fresh use—if moderate, so much the more weighty and effective. Such passages, therefore, are very conspicuous, and may very well have made a decided impression on Melville and have provoked him to imitation." (Weber, *Stilistische Untersuchung*, p. 106.)

88.  *White Jacket*, p. 212; "Paradise of Bachelors," XIII, 230–231.

89.  *P.R.*, IV, 34–38.

90.  Havens, *Influence of Milton*, p. 84.

91.  See, for example, *Mardi*, I, 267–268; II, 336–337; *White Jacket*, pp. 262–263; *Moby-Dick*, I, 165; *Clarel*, I, 293.

> *The medium of . . .* [Melville's] *philosophical romances, particularly* Moby-Dick, *is a distinctive epic prose that is indebted to the English stylists of the seventeenth century. Characteristic of their prose and of Melville's is a richness of allusion to matters historical, geographical, and philosophical that demonstrates wide reading and informative conversation on the part of the author.* [*Sealts*, Melville's Reading in Ancient Philosophy, *p. 23.*]

92. *Moby-Dick*, II, 101–104.

93. *Mardi*, II, 199.

94. *P.L.*, IV, 268–285.

95. Weber, *Stilistische Untersuchung*, p. 86; Havens, *Influence of Milton*, p. 81. For examples, see *Moby-Dick*, II, 197–201, 205–207, 224–226, 249, etc.; *Journal up the Straits*, p. 78; *P.L.*, II, 346, 470, 552–557, 769, 790, 921; V, 645–650, etc.

96. Havens, *Influence of Milton*, p. 81. For examples, see omission of *of*, *Moby-Dick*, I, 42 and *P.L.*, III, 71, etc.; omission of *a*, *Confidence-Man*, p. 47 and *P.L.*, IX, 494–495; omission of verb, *Moby-Dick*, I, 298, II, 248 and *P.L.*, I, 140–142, IX, 912–913; and *Moby-Dick*, II, 171–172 and *P.L.*, IX, 792.

97. Addison, *Spectator*, No. CCLXXXV, pp. 35–36. Italics in original.

98. Havens, *Influence of Milton*, pp. 80–81.

99. *P.L.*, VII, 2, 17; IX, 457–458; X, 366.

100. *Mardi*, I, 37, 43; *Moby-Dick*, II, 111, 207. See also Appendix B.

101. *Mardi*, II, 272; *P.L.*, VI, 82.

102. *Redburn*, p. 323; *P.L.*, II, 628. *Dire* is postpositional also in *P.L.*, VI, 665, 766; X, 524; XI, 474; XII, 175.

103. *Moby-Dick*, I, 236; *P.L.*, III, 72. *Sublime* appears to be postpositional also in *P.L.*, II, 528; IV, 300; VIII, 455; in some of these cases, including that quoted here, careful reading shows that *sublime* actually modifies a noun other than the one it follows.

104. *Pierre*, p. 26; *P.L.*, IX, 910. See also *Clarel*, II, 170; "Il Penseroso," 1. 119.

105. *Clarel*, II, 257.

106. Postpositional adjectives, inverted subjects and predicates, and inverted objects and verbs seem to be unusually numerous in *Mardi*.

107. *Moby-Dick*, I, 296; "The Conflict of Convictions," *Battle-Pieces*, XVI, 10; *P.L.*, VI, 369–370; II, 703.

108. *Moby-Dick*, II, 175, 245; *P.L.*, X, 22–23.

109. *Moby-Dick*, II, 189, 233; *P.L.*, IV, 32; V, 332.

110. *Mardi*, I, 29; II, 289; *P.L.*, XII, 610; V, 210.

111. *P.L.*, I, 775–777; II, 417, 499; III, 345–347; VI, 257–260, etc. Cf. *Mardi*, I, 20; II, 120; *Moby-Dick*, II, 39, 318.

112. Hanford, *Milton Handbook*, p. 299.

113. *P.L.*, I, 192–196; IX, 634–640.

114. *Moby-Dick*, I, 241–242.

115. Weber, *Stilistische Untersuchung*, p. 73. See also *Billy Budd*, ed. Freeman, pp. 103 ff.

116. Weber, for example, makes much of Donne in his sections on "Literarische Beeinflussung" and "Abhängigkeit" (*Stilistische Untersuchung*, pp. 34, 57, 86, 94, etc.), yet in his "Chronologische Folge der Hinweise" and "Literarische Hinweise"

143

(*Ibid.*, pp. 11–13, 201–205) there is no mention of Donne. I know of no evidence that Melville knew even the name of John Donne.

117. *Pierre*, ed. Robert S. Forsythe (N.Y., 1930), pp. xxxvi–xxxvii.

118. Mansfield, *Melville*, p. 199.

119. See Chapter VII. In this connection Nathalia Wright remarks,

> The extent of . . . [*Melville's*] *knowledge of Browne, Donne, Bunyan, Milton is as yet undetermined, but the Biblical overtones of their prose are unmistakable to even a cursory reader. Falling as they habitually do into Scriptural idiom, these writers represent a stylistic rather than a doctrinal transmission of the Scriptures.* [Biblical Allusion in the Prose of Herman Melville (*unpublished M.A. essay in Yale University Library, 1938*), *pp. 74–75.*]

Because of their quotations, paraphrases, and parallels of Scripture, *Paradise Lost* and other of Milton's poems provide as good a vehicle as his prose—if not a better one—for the transmission of Biblical style.

# Chapter Four
### [Pages 50–63]

1. H.M. to Richard H. Dana, Jr., May 1, 1850 (Harrison Hayford, "Two New Letters of Herman Melville," *Journal of English Literary History*, XI [March, 1944], 76–83; p. 79).

2. *Moby-Dick*, II, 184.

3. John Erskine, *The Delight of Great Books* (Indianapolis, 1928), pp. 230, 223.

4. Sealts, *Melville's Reading in Ancient Philosophy*, p. 23; Mumford, *Melville*, p. 181; *Pierre*, ed. Forsythe, p. xxxii; *Billy Budd*, ed. Freeman, p. 73.

5. Padraic Colum, *A Half-Day's Ride* (N.Y., 1932), pp. 175–176.

6. *E.g.*, James Holly Hanford, "The Dramatic Element in *Paradise Lost*," *Studies in Philology*, XIV (April, 1917), 178–195; Matthiessen, *American Renaissance*, pp. 414–421.

7. Addison, *Spectator*, No. CCCXV, p. 72.

8. *Moby-Dick*, II, 335; I, 44, 293. Weber calls the last quotation "epischer Prosa" (*Stilistische Untersuchung*, p. 17).

9. *Redburn*, p. 323.

10. Weber, *Stilistische Untersuchung*, pp. 34–35.

11. *E.g.*, George C. Homans, "The Dark Angel: The Tragedy of Herman Melville," *New England Quarterly*, V (October, 1932), 699–730; p. 715: "At times, like its companions, *Moby-Dick* seeks the level of blank verse rhapsody."

12. Matthiessen, *American Renaissance*, p. 426. Padraic Colum has analyzed and printed other passages as "conventionally epical . . . prose," blank verse, polyphonic prose, and free verse (*Half-Day's Ride*, pp. 176–179).

13. *Moby-Dick*, II, 257. Here and below I have capitalized the initial letters of the "lines."

14. Weber, *Stilistische Untersuchung*, p. 22.

*Master as . . . [Milton] was of all the resources of verse, he was less an innovator in "numbers" than in other things. Every important characteristic of his versification which is capable of being defined, isolated, and catalogued is to be found in the plays of Shakespeare and the lesser Elizabethans [Havens, Influence of Milton, p. 86].*

15. Particularly the examples just referred to in Matthiessen.

16. H.M. to E.A.D., February 24, 1849 (*Selections*, ed. Thorp, p. 370).

17. *Mardi*, I, [vii].

18. Minnigerode, *Personal Letters of Melville*, pp. 137–138.

19. *Mardi*, II, 272. Iambic rhythm immediately precedes and follows this selection, and occurs elsewhere in *Mardi* (II, 54, 120, 375–377).

20. Addison, *Spectator*, No. CCCIII, p. 58. Italics in original.

21. *Moby-Dick*, II, 318.

22. Four extended similes for a frigate are presented in succession in *White Jacket*, pp. 94–95.

23. *Moby-Dick*, II, 343–344.

24. *Ibid.*, I, 54; II, 97, 263, 345. *P.L.*, I, 594 ff., 768 ff.

25. *Moby-Dick*, I, 344, 346–347; II, 127; *Clarel*, II, 75. *P.L.*, I, 203 ff., 230 ff., 287 ff., 302 ff., 338 ff.; IV, 159 ff.

*Melville's pronounced poetic and impressionistic comparisons from nature and animal life unite him with romanticism, while his many geographic, historic, folk-loric, Biblical, and mythological comparisons indicate a continuation of the rhetorical tradition of the Renaissance (Rabelais, Lyly, Shakespeare, Marlowe, Milton; also Carlyle) [Weber, Stilistische Untersuchung, p. 139].*

26. Matthiessen, *American Renaissance*, p. 461. Italics in original.

27. *Moby-Dick*, II, 284. The last four lines present, of course, some unimportant variations from a strict iambic pentameter pattern.

28. *P.L.*, I, 609–615. See also James Whaler, "The Miltonic Simile," *Publications of the Modern Language Association*, XLVI (December, 1931), 1034–1074.

29. N. Bryllion Fagin, "Herman Melville and the Interior Monologue," *Am. Lit.*, VI (January, 1935), 433–434; p. 433.

30. *P.L.*, IV, 32 ff.; IX, 99 ff., 794 ff., 896 ff.

31. *Ibid.*, IX, 895.

32. *Ibid.*, VIII, 57–58; XI, 754, 273–274.

33. *Moby-Dick*, I, 44, 183; II, 281.

34. Weber, *Stilistische Untersuchung*, pp. 127–128. On p. 176 Weber mentions again "das wuchtige Pathos Miltons."

35. Nor should it be forgotten that other of Melville's works bear incidental like-

nesses to Milton's epic. In *Mardi* (II, 120), for example, Melville introduces a speech with this sentence fragment of ablative absolutes:

*Some remedies applied, and the company grown composed, Babbalanja thus. . . .*
Milton also introduced speeches with sentence fragments and *thus* (*P.L.*, IV, 610, 634, 834, 885, etc.).

36. *Moby-Dick*, I, 76, 81, 85, 100; *P.L.*, III.

37. Addison, *Spectator*, No. CCXCVII, pp. 46–47. A more charitable view is implied in No. CCCXXXIII, p. 100.

38. Lascelles Abercrombie, *The Epic* (London, [1914]), p. 52. This book is the basis for much of the following discussion.

39. *Ibid.*, pp. 39, 45.

40. Pommer, "Melville and the Wake of the *Essex*," pp. 290–292.

41. Charles Olson, *Call Me Ishmael* (N.Y., [1947]), pp. 16–25; Sedgwick, *Melville*, pp. 89–91; Weaver, *Melville*, pp. 135–159.

42. Abercrombie, *Epic*, p. 39. Cf. More, "The Theme of *Paradise Lost*," p. 239: "An epic . . . must be built upon a theme deeply rooted in national belief."

43. *Ibid.*, p. 42.

44. *Ibid.*, pp. 17, 39, 69–70. Cf. More, "The Theme of *Paradise Lost*," pp. 239–240: "The development of . . . [an epic] theme must express, more or less symbolically, some universal truth of human nature. . . . The poet himself need not be fully conscious of this deeper meaning."

45. John Freeman, *Herman Melville* (N.Y., 1926), pp. 116–117.

46. Abercrombie, *Epic*, p. 80.

47. *Ibid.*, pp. 50, 13, 12, 7.

48. *Ibid.*, p. 39.

49. Havens, *Influence of Milton*, pp. 85, 80–85, 80.

50. *Moby-Dick*, II, 38, 366.

51. Rosenbach, *An Introduction to . . . Moby-Dick*, p. 6.

52. Matthiessen, *American Renaissance*, p. 122.

53. Addison, *Spectator*, No. CCCXXXIX, p. 102.

54. Hanford, *Milton Handbook*, pp. 293–294.

55. Addison, *Spectator*, No. CCCXXVII, p. 90; italics in original.

# Chapter Five
[Pages 64–80]

1. *P.L.*, III, 686–689.

2. *Confidence-Man*, p. 173.

3. *Typee*, p. 122.

4. "Encantadas," X, 185.

5. *Redburn*, p. 324; cf. *P.L.*, V, 255; VII, 207.

6. *White Jacket*, p. 146.

7. "Encantadas," X, 199.

8. *P.L.*, I, 741; V, 758–759; II, 1047–1049; I, 177; VII, 234. Cf. VII, 168.

9. *Mardi*, II, 332; *Moby-Dick*, I, 164; *Pierre*, p. 149; *Clarel*, II, 4; and "The New Ancient of Days," XVI, 409.

10. *P.L.*, II, 901, 963–967.

11. "New Zealot to the Sun," *Timoleon*, XVI, 265. Where Chaos had been, Earth came to be, and Milton's "verdurous wall" and "highest wall" of Paradise (*P.L.*, IV, 143, 182) may have suggested the imagery of a sentence in *Clarel* (I, 175):

> High walled,
> An Eden owned he nigh his town,
> Which locked in leafy emerald
> A frescoed lodge.

12. *P.L.*, X, 304–305.

13. *Journal up the Straits*, pp. 140, 164. Milton described Hell as containing sulphur, and Moloch threatened that God should see

> his throne itself
> Mix'd with Tartarean sulphur
> [P.L., *I, 69, 674; II, 68–69*].

This last line may have caused the association of two of its words in Melville's "classification of the constituents of a chaos"—his chapter on cetology:

> CHAPTER VI. (Sulphur-bottom).—*Another retiring gentleman, with a brimstone belly, doubtless got by scraping along the* Tartarian *tiles in some of his profounder divings* [Moby-Dick, *I, 164, 173;* Sulphur-bottom *italicized in original*].

There is similar vaguely Miltonic writing in "The Two Temples" (XIII, 184) during a description of London:

> The fiendish *gas-lights shooting their* Tartarean *rays across the muddy, sticky streets, lit up the pitiless and pitiable scene. . . . Disentangling myself at last from those skeins of* Pandemonian *lanes . . . I found myself . . . in a wide and far less noisy street.*

14. *P.L.*, X, 550–551, 560–567.

15. Todd's note to *P.L.*, X, 561 ff., reads in part as follows (italics in original): ✓

> *The Dead Sea, or the lake* Asphaltites, *so called from the* bitumen *which it is said to have cast up: near which* Sodom *and* Gomorrah *were situated. Josephus mentions the* apples of Sodom *as dissolving into ashes and smoke at the first touch. But our countrymen, Sandys and Maundrell, who visited the Holy Land, are inclined to disbelieve that such fruit existed. . . . See also* Sir John Maundeville's Travels . . . *where he is speaking of this delusive fruit,* [and Cotovicus].

Melville may, of course, have been impressed by some account of the apples of

Sodom other than Milton's, but this seems unlikely to me. Of the four treatments which Todd mentions, Josephus and Mandeville are mentioned only once each in Melville's works (*Clarel*, I, 216 and *Mardi*, I, 346); Cotovicus, not at all. Sandys and Maundrell he may have known somewhat more intimately (Walter E. Bezanson, *Herman Melville's "Clarel,"* unpublished dissertation in Yale University Library, 1943, pp. 142–143, 346–348).

16. *Typee*, pp. 70–71. Milton had used *element* to refer to water in *P.L.*, VIII, 348.

17. *Moby-Dick*, II, 330.

18. *Confidence-Man*, p. 225.

19. *P.L.*, IX, 578. Cf. IX, 577–578; X, 550–551.

20. *Clarel*, I, 290.

21. In describing the Dead Sea, he recorded

> *old boughs tossed up by water—relics of pick-nick—nought to eat but bitumen & ashes with desert of Sodom apples washed down with water of Dead Sea* [Journal up the Straits, *pp. 74–75; cf. p. 73*].

22. "Encantadas," X, 185, 183.

23. *P.L.*, X, 573.

24. "Encantadas," X, 183–184. The contrast in the last quotation occurs also *Ibid.*, p. 246; in *Pierre*, p. 58; and in Melville's title "The Paradise of Bachelors and the Tartarus of Maids," XIII, 228. Milton used *Tartarus* as synonymous with *Hell* in *P.L.*, II, 858; VI, 54. Similarities between "Sketch First" of "Encantadas" and *P.L.* were pointed out by Miss Hunter (*Herman Melville's Sketches and Tales*, pp. 60–62). Although Miss Hunter pointed out that Milton called Pandemonium a "Plutonian hall" (*P.L.*, X, 444), she did not mention that one of Melville's sources described part of the Encantadas as "a shore fit for Pandemonium" (Robert Fitzroy, quoted in Anderson, *Melville in the South Seas*, p. 51).

25. Sundermann has suggested (*Melvilles Gedankengut*, p. 202, n. 46) a comparison between these two passages:

> *In his faculties, high Oro is but what a man would be, infinitely magnified* [Mardi, *II, 123*].

> *Wir fühlen deutlich, wie die Versuche Miltons, Gott menschliche Vernunftgrund-sätze aufzuzwingen, notwendig in der Begrenzung göttlicher Absolutheit enden müssen* [Hans-Oskar Wilde, Der Gottesgedanke in der englischen Literatur (*Breslau, 1930*), p. 52].

26. *Mardi*, I, 268.

27. *P.L.*, VII, 166–169. Sundermann cited the passage from *Mardi* as related to Plato's *Timaeus* (*Melvilles Gedankengut*, p. 94, n. 62), and Sealts showed its relationship to Milton (*Melville's Reading in Ancient Philosophy*, pp. 109–110). On the latter page Sealts suggested a comparison between "the image in *Mardi* of God moving on the face of the waters," and *Pierre*, p. 284, the last of which "seems to recall both" the Bible and Milton (*Genesis*, i, 2; *P.L.*, I, 19 ff.). The similarity to Milton seems to me to be remote.

28. *Mardi*, II, 352.

29. *Moby-Dick*, I, 5.

30. *P.L.*, V, 300–311; IX, 403.

31. *White Jacket*, p. 35.

32. *P.L.*, IV, 288–290, 300–301.

33. *Moby-Dick*, I, 237–238.

34. See the quotation from Boynton in n. 42 to Chapter I.

35. *P.L.*, IX, 394–396; IV, 268–271, 274–275.

36. *Mardi*, II, 268. The next sentence is this:

> *Artless airs came from the shore; and from the censer-swinging roses, a* bloom, as *if from* Hebe's cheek.

Here another collocation of words is subject to Miltonic attribution, because of

> *Nods, and Becks, and wreathed Smiles,*
> *Such* as *hang on* Hebe's cheek
> [*"L'Allegro," ll. 28–29*]

and

> *Were they of manly prime, or youthful* bloom?
> As *smooth* as Hebe's *their unrazor'd lips*
> [Comus, *ll. 289–300*].

37. "To Our Queen," XVI, 342. Melville italicized *you.*

38. *P.L.*, XI, 273–282.

39. Except for Moloch, who is discussed near the end of this chapter, none of Satan's followers in *P.L.* appears clearly in Melville. When *Belial* is used ("The Armies of the Wilderness," *Battle-Pieces*, XVI, 69), the name seems to signify Satan, not a follower of Satan; and I cannot see much value in Sundermann's suggestion (*Melvilles Gedankengut*, pp. 203, 208) that with the passage describing Sin and Death in *P.L.* (II, 770 ff.) one should compare Melville's statement that "Sin is death" (*Mardi*, II, 376). The variety of occupations which Milton's devils find when Satan leaves for Earth (*P.L.*, II, 521–628) might possibly have suggested to Melville this simile in *White Jacket* (p. 341):

> '*You're merry, my boy,*' *said Jack, looking up with a glance like that of a sentimental archangel doomed to drag out his eternity in disgrace.*

40. *Clarel*, II, 45. *Tartarus* is mentioned on the same page, another instance of its occurring near Miltonic material with which it seems linked by association.

41. Melville's "in the sun" occurs in Milton's description of Satan's seeing

> *within ken a glorious* Angel stand,
> *The same whom John saw also* in the sun
> [*P.L., III, 622–623*].

Milton had borrowed, in turn, from *Revelation*, xix, 17: "And I saw an *angel standing in the sun*." This example raises another instance of a problem mentioned earlier— is a given passage Miltonic or Biblical in its literary background? The doubtful lines in this case are

> *The* Victory, *whose Admiral,*

> *With orders nobly won,*
> *Shone in the globe of the battle glow—*
> The angel in that sun
> ["*The* Temeraire," Battle-Pieces, *XVI, 42*; Victory *italicized in original*].

42.  H.M. to E.A.D., February 24, 1849 (*Selections,* ed. Thorp, p. 370).

43.  *Moby-Dick,* I, xii. *Seven-storied* may be an unconscious recall of *P.L.,* III, 481–482:

> *They pass the planets seven, and pass the fix'd,*
> *And that crystalline sphere.* . . .

44.  *Mardi,* I, 213. Cf. the drawing, *Satan Exalted Sat.*

45.  *Ibid.,* I, 344; II, 270.

46.  *Confidence-Man,* p. 263.

47.  *P.L.,* VIII, 217.

48.  *Clarel,* II, 148. Milton, of course, had written that "Spirits, when they please,/ Can either sex assume, or both" (*P.L.,* I, 423–424).

49.  *Ibid.,* V, 275–287.

50.  "The Marquis de Grandvin," XIII, 351.

51.  *P.L.,* VII, 40–42. Cf. Adam to Raphael (VIII, 648–649):

> *Gentle to me and* affable *hath been*
> *Thy condescension.*

52.  H.M. to Catherine Gansevoort Lansing, August, 1875 (*Family Correspondence of Herman Melville, 1830–1904,* ed. Victor Hugo Paltsits [N.Y., 1929], p. 33). Cf. Adam to Michael:

> True *opener of mine eyes, prime Angel blest.* . . .
> *Now first I find*
> *My eyes* true-*opening, and my heart much eas'd*
> [P.L., *XI, 598; XII, 273–274*].

53.  Francis Parkman, *The California and Oregon Trail* (N.Y., 1849), p. 35.

54.  Melville, "Mr. Parkman's Tour," *The Literary World,* IV (March 31, 1849), 291–293; p. 292.

55.  *P.L.,* VI, 332–333.

56.  *White Jacket,* p. 206.

57.  *Israel Potter,* p. 161. Italics in original.

58.  "The Piazza," X, 7.

59.  *Clarel,* II, 93.

60.  *P.L.,* VI, 202–203.

61.  "Cock-A-Doodle-Doo!" XIII, 145, 146, 150, 158.

62.  *P.L.,* II, 618–621. A somewhat less Miltonic series occurs later in "Cock-A-Doodle-Doo!" (XIII, 152):

*Plainly, Shanghai was of the opinion that duns only came into the world to be kicked, hanged, bruised, battered, choked, walloped, hammered, drowned, clubbed!*

63.　Pp. 33; 68; 147, n. 13; 148, n. 24; 149, n. 40.

64.　*Leviticus*, xviii, 21; *I Kings*, xi, 5; *II Kings*, xxiii, 10; *Zephaniah*, i, 5; *Acts*, vii, 43.

65.　In his note to 1. 205 of "On the Morning of Christ's Nativity" Todd quotes "Sandys's *Travels*, p. 186. edit. 1615. fol." on the trumpets and timbrels used by the priests of Moloch.

66.　*P.L.*, I, 392–396.

67.　"On the Morning of Christ's Nativity," 11. 205–210.

68.　It is probably not important that Melville's desire for "fifty conspiring mountains" to crush the engine bears remote analogy to the mountains which the angels hurl on Satan's artillery (*P.L.*, VI, 637–666), and that on p. 149 of "Cock-A-Doodle-Doo!" Melville mentions "Mile-End," the name which Milton prominently splits between lines 7 and 8 of "On the Detractions. . . . "

69.　Milton uses *vernal* in *P.L.*, III, 43; IV, 155, 264; etc.

70.　Here, as elsewhere in Milton and Melville, a hyphen is omitted between two words so linked as normally to require one.

71.　*S.A.*, 1. 1346.

72.　*P.L.*, VIII, 332–333; IX, 11. Cf. p. 35 above.

73.　*Battle-Pieces*, XVI, [3].

74.　"The Conflict of Convictions," *Battle-Pieces*, XVI, 8–9.

75.　"A Canticle," *Ibid.*, p. 100. The first of these quotations from "A Canticle" seems to reflect Satan's statement,

> *The fiery surge, that from the* precipice
> *Of Heaven receiv'd us* falling; *and the* thunder
> *Wing'd with red lightning and impetuous rage,*
> *Perhaps hath spent his shafts, and ceases now*
> *To bellow through the vast and boundless* deep.
> (P.L., *I, 173–177*).

76.　Cf. "Is Satan weak?" (*Clarel*, II, 246).

77.　Cf. "sage white-robed Truth" ("On the Death of a Fair Infant," 1. 54) and "white-handed Hope" (*Comus*, 1. 213).

78.　*P.L.*, I, 679–684.

79.　*P.L.*, I, 192–193. Melville may have described the Giant of the Pool as having a "forehead white as wool" because of the suggestiveness of whiteness discussed in Chapter XLII of *Moby-Dick*, or because of the white bubbles surrounding a whale when one heaves its forehead.

80.　"Apathy and Enthusiasm," *Battle-Pieces*, XVI, 12. The lines following those quoted are these:

> *And at the towers of Erebus*
> *Our striplings flung the scoff.*

"Erebus" introduces Hellenic imagery to a predominantly Hebraic environment.

151

Here and elsewhere Melville mixes Hellenic and Hebraic mythology as Milton did.

A reference to Michael which does not seem very Miltonic occurs in "The Battle for the Mississippi," *Battle-Pieces*, XVI, 47:

> *a war*
> *Like Michael's waged with leven.*

81. "The Fall of Richmond," *Battle-Pieces*, XVI, 98. We should probably be reminded of Satan the threatener of Gabriel:

> *On the other side, Satan, alarm'd,*
> *Collecting all his might, dilated stood, . . .*
> *His stature reach'd the sky, and on his crest*
> *Sat Horrour plum'd*
> [P.L., *IV, 985–989*].

Melville may well have thought that Grant was a modern Gabriel.

82. "The Armies of the Wilderness," *Battle-Pieces*, XVI, 69. The lines are in italics in the original. Cf. *P.L.*, II, 112–115, 226; Melville probably had in mind Belial's method of persuasion, not his specific recommendations.

83. "The March Into Virginia," *Battle-Pieces*, XVI, 13. This poem immediately follows "Apathy and Enthusiasm."

# Chapter Six
[Pages 81–104]

1. *Mardi*, II, 359.

2. *Pierre*, p. 82.

3. *Redburn*, pp. 356–357.

4. *Confidence-Man*, p. 317. See p. 112 above.

5. The evidence of this chapter will serve to support a generalization implied in one of Nathalia Wright's conclusions:

> *In the matter of characterization Melville is indebted to the Bible for certain proto-types. . . . [But] however distinctly they may stand in the relation of prototypes to Melville's characters, none of these Biblical personalities is in any sense the basis for an allegory. Elaborate symbol and detailed parallel was foreign to Melville's genius; his was a gothic not a classic method. Of all the analogies suggested by Biblical characters none is completely conceived and perfectly carried out. Only a hint is given, a tradition implied; upon complete application the pattern breaks down.* ["*Biblical Allusion in Melville's Prose*," pp. 187, 190.]

6. A. Melville assures us that in heaven we shall

> *list to no shallow gossip of Magellans and Drakes; but give ear to the voyagers who have circumnavigated the* Ecliptic; *who* rounded *the* Polar Star *as Cape Horn.*
> [Mardi, *I, 14.*]

One such far voyager was he who stood

> *on the lower stair*
> *That scal'd by steps of gold to heaven-gate. . . .*
> Round *he surveys . . . from eastern point*
> *Of Libra to the fleecy* star *that bears*
> *Andromeda far off Atlantick seas*
> *Beyond the horizon; then from* pole *to* pole
> *He views in breadth, and without longer pause*
> *Down right into the world's first region throws*
> *His flight precipitant, and winds with ease*
> *Through the pure marble air his oblique way*
> *Amongst innumerable stars. . . .*
> *Down from the* ecliptick, [*he*] *sped with hop'd success.*
> [P.L., *III, 540–541, 555–565, 740.*]

B. See n. 44 of preceding chapter.

C. *Mardi*, II, 1 (discussed briefly in Hillway, "Taji's Quest for Certainty," p. 27).

D. *Israel Potter*, p. 167 (not in Melville's source for *Israel Potter;* possibly from *P.L.*, I, 533–539; V, 701).

E. In a lecture Melville talked of devilfish, and "drew a most fearfully unfavorable picture for his Satanic fishship" (*The Daily Wisconsin* [Milwaukee], February 26, 1859, p. 1; quoted in Merrell R. Davis, "Melville's Midwestern Lecture Tour, 1859," *Philological Quarterly*, XX [January, 1941], 46–57; p. 49).

F. *Clarel*, I, 189; cf. *P.L.*, I, VI; *P.R.*, III, 308–309.

7. *White Jacket*, p. 245. Phlegethon forms part of the geography of Milton's Hell (*P.L.*, II, 580); note the Miltonic flavor of the end of the sentence which follows the quotation from *White Jacket*:

> *In some cases, a man, hurled thus from a yard, has fallen upon his own ship-mates in the tops, and dragged them down with him to the same destruction with himself.*

8. *Confidence-Man*, p. 251.

9. *P.L.*, IX, 496–525. The fact that rattlesnakes are not gold adds to the probability that Melville had Satan and not real snakes in mind in the prose passage (Elizabeth Foster, *Herman Melville's "The Confidence Man"* unpublished dissertation in Yale University Library, 1942, p. 186). Miss Foster points out some of the above similarities in wording and concludes that "the similarity between Melville's and Milton's descriptions is probably not accidental, especially . . . since Melville had already equated the Confidence-Man with the devil in making the gimlet-eyed cynic ask: 'How much money did the devil make by gulling Eve [*Confidence-Man*, p. 42]?'" Cf. the descriptions of serpents in *Redburn*, pp. 297, 303.

10. *Typee*, p. 115.

11. *Billy-Budd*, XIII, 31.

12. *Clarel*, I, 108, 152.

13. *P.L.*, XI, 614, 616–617.

14. Percy Bysshe Shelley, *Shelley Memorials*, ed. Lady Shelley (Boston, 1859), p. 245. Melville's copy is in the Houghton Library.

15. *P.L.*, IX, 351–352, and passages shortly to be referred to; *Areopagitica*, I, 173, 177.

16. *Mardi*, II, 301. Cf. *Ibid.*, II, 156, where Babbalanja explains man's moral sense to Media, the demigod. There Melville writes of passions and the moral sense in a way slightly suggestive of Milton, but much more suggestive of the psychology of Anthony Cooper, third Earl of Shaftesbury; Francis Hutcheson; and David Hartley.

17. Pope is prominent among these, both because of Epistle II of his *Essay on Man*, and because of Melville's acquaintance with his writing (shown, in part, in *Omoo*, p. 211; *White Jacket*, p. 266; *Moby-Dick*, I, xvii; and "I and My Chimney," XIII, 288). A sentence from Matthiessen is pertinent here (*American Renaissance*, p. 308): "In depicting both Hester's wild grief in prison and her almost mad joy of release in the forest, Hawthorne was again subscribing to Milton's understanding of the way in which passion could drive out the faculty of reason, and wrongfully usurp its place."

18. *P.L.*, XII, 86–92; cf. *P.R.*, II, 466–472.

19. *Moby-Dick*, I, 231, 232, 210; cf. I, 252; II, 41.

20. *Billy Budd*, XIII, 46.

21. *P.L.*, IX, 1127–1131. At one point in *Moby-Dick* (II, 16) Melville uses one aspect of the reason-passion problem for humor. Fleece preaches to hundreds of sharks:

> *Your woraciousness, fellow-critters, I don't blame ye so much for; dat is natur, and can't be helped; but to gobern dat wicked natur, dat is de pint. You is sharks, sartin; but if you gobern de shark in you, why den you be angel; for all angel is not'ing more dan de shark well goberned.*

This should be compared with *P.L.*, V, 482–490.

22. R. E. Watters, "Melville's 'Sociality,' " *Am. Lit.*, XVII (March, 1945), 33–49; p. 45.

23. *Redburn*, pp. 72, 356, 356–357, 74 (italics in original), 76.

24. *P.L.*, IX, 119–130.

25. *Redburn*, p. 134.

26. *Moby-Dick*, I, 206.

27. *Redburn*, p. 77; cf. pp. 72, 355, 381.

28. *Journal up the Straits*, p. 145.

29. *White Jacket*, pp. 232, 233. "The monster of Sin itself" and "Tophet," further Miltonic links, are mentioned on pp. 230, 231. The ellipsis in the latest quotation in the text concerns Goethe's Margaret and Devil, but I believe that I am not suppressing unfavorable evidence. Melville's sentence before the ellipsis may allude to Mephistopheles, but the following ones point more towards Satan.

30. *P.L.*, IX, 354, 492.

31. *White Jacket*, p. 234.

32. *P.L.*, VI, 181.

33. *Billy Budd*, XIII, 45, 49.

34. *Ibid.*, pp. 61, 49. Cf. Charles R. Anderson, "The Genesis of *Billy Budd*," *Am. Lit.*, XII (November, 1940), 329–346; p. 335: Claggart's "sadistic nature could not rest until it played the serpent to this young Adam"—Billy Budd.

35. *Billy Budd*, XIII, 16, 17, 18.

36. *Ibid.*, p. 48. Allusions to Satan follow fast upon the use of this quotation.

37. *P.L.*, IV, 115.

38. The ideas of "The Whiteness of the Whale" in *Moby-Dick* may have had as much influence here as did "*Pale* ire." Cf. the suggestiveness of *Bland*.

39. "To characterize what Claggart feels, Melville has recourse to the quotation, 'Pale ire, envy, and despair,' the forces that were working in Milton's Satan as he first approached the Garden of Eden." (Matthiessen, *American Renaissance*, p. 505.)

40. *Billy Budd*, XIII, 48–49, 60.

41. *P.L.*, IV, 358–392.

42. Cf. *Billy Budd*, ed. Freeman, pp. 54 ff.

43. *P.L.*, IV, 73–74.

44. *Billy Budd*, XIII, 31, 32, 61.

45. *P.L.*, VI, 734–741; IX, 692–697.

46. Bush, *Paradise Lost*, pp. 62–74; C. S. Lewis, *A Preface to Paradise Lost* (London, 1942); Abercrombie, *Epic*, pp. 157–158.

47. *Pierre*, p. 248.

48. William S. Gleim, *The Meaning of Moby-Dick* (N.Y., 1938), p. 123.

49. Carl Van Doren, "Lucifer from Nantucket," *Century Magazine*, CX (August, 1925), 494–501; p. 497.

50. Sedgwick, *Melville*, p. 145.

51. Weber, *Stilistische Untersuchung*, p. 186.

52. Murray, "Personality and Creative Imagination," p. 158. Cf. Matthiessens' statement that the soliloquies of *Moby-Dick* sometimes show a bad "romantic Satanism" (*American Renaissance*, p. 460). Links between Ahab and Satan are developed in Viola Chittenden White, *Symbolism in Herman Melville's Writings* (unpublished dissertation in University of North Carolina Library, 1934), pp. 165–178, 334–338.

53. *Moby-Dick*, I, 10. There may be a connection between this description and Melville's print, *Satan Exalted Sat*.

54. *White Jacket*, pp. 9, 85.

55. *Moby-Dick*, I, 81.

56. *Ibid.*, I, 152–153; II, 281.

57. *P.L.*, I, 600–601. Thorp believes that a scarred tree in Pittsfield suggested Ahab's scar (*Moby-Dick*, ed. Willard Thorp [N.Y., 1947], p. 114).

58. *Moby-Dick*, I, 291; II, 55–58, 116, 122. Cf. *P.L.*, I, 221–224.

59. *Moby-Dick*, II, 190. " 'As proud as Lucifer'—a conventional simile, to be sure; but Melville, like his hero, admired the rebel archangel for his proud and heroic defiance" (Geist, *Melville*, p. 51).

60. *Moby-Dick*, II, 231. *Synod* is one of Milton's words for an assembly of good or bad angels (*P.L.*, II, 391, etc.).

61. *P.L.*, I, 315. Cf. Satan's words to and about his followers in *P.R.*, II, 124; IV, 201: "Powers *of fire*," and "Tetrarchs *of fire*."

62. *Moby-Dick*, II, 283.

63. *P.L.*, XII, 491–492; cf. VI, 213; *P.R.*, IV, 424.

64. *Moby-Dick*, II, 328, 330, 354, 360, 367, 261. With the next to the last of these, cf. *Redburn*, p. 356:

> *I can never think of [Jackson] . . . but I am reminded of . . . the diabolical Tiberius at Capreae; who . . . endeavoured to drag down with him to his own perdition all who came within the evil spell of his power.*

65. H.M. to Nathaniel Hawthorne, June 29, 1851 (Julian Hawthorne, *Nathaniel Hawthorne and His Wife* [Boston, 1885], 2 vols., I, 400).

66. Consider, for example, H.M. to Nathaniel Hawthorne, August 16, 1851 (Weaver, *Melville*, p. 316):

> *By usable truth, we mean the apprehension of the absolute condition of present things as they strike the eye of the man who fears them not, though they do their worst to him,—the man who, like Russia or the British Empire, declares himself a sovereign nature (in himself) amid the Powers of heaven, hell, and earth. He may perish; but so long as he exists he insists upon treating with all powers upon an equal basis. [Cf. P.L., I, 258–263]*

67. Bush, *Paradise Lost*, p. 52: "The theme of *Paradise Lost* is the conflict between human pride and religious humility."

68. *Moby-Dick*, II, 298, 239; cf. II, 190.

69. *P.L.*, I, 56–58; IV, 38–40; cf. I, 36, 527, 572, 603; etc.

70. Lewis, *Paradise Lost*, p. 55.

71. *P.L.*, V, 664–665; I, 98.

72. *P.L.*, I, 54–55.

73. "The tyrant of Milton's poem, as some readers have seen, is not God but Satan" (Bush, *Paradise Lost*, p. 72). Certainly the tyrant of *Moby-Dick* is Ahab, not the White Whale.

74. *Moby-Dick*, I, 211. Cf. *Redburn*, p. 75: "It is not for me to say what it was that made a whole ship's company submit so to the whims of one poor miserable man like Jackson. I only know that so it was."

75. Addison, *Spectator*, No. CCCIX, p. 59.

76. Homans, "The Dark Angel: The Tragedy of Herman Melville," p. 728. Another discussion of Ahab's sacrilege may be found in Reginald L. Cook, "Big Medicine in 'Moby-Dick,' " *Accent*, VIII (Winter, 1948), 102–109.

77. *Moby-Dick*, I, 116, 210. Cf. Ahab's defiance of the corposants, II, 281–282, and *Pierre*, p. 150.

78. *P.L.*, II, 46–48; V, 725–726; I, 40; IX, 125.

79. *Moby-Dick*, I, 204, 211.

80. *Ibid.*, I, 229–230.

81. Freeman, *Melville*, p. 116.

82. Henry Alonzo Myers, *Are Men Equal?* (N.Y., 1945), p. 189:

> *Possessed by his one idea of striking through Moby-Dick to the source of evil, he nevertheless feels that he is acting against the will of God. Feeling that his central impulse comes from the devil, he proposes to be the devil's child, not serenely if it must be so, . . . but with a delirious bravado.*

83. White, *Symbolism in Melville*, p. 172: "The White Whale is used by Melville as a symbol of the Old Testament Jehovah . . . as a primitive force, not in his fatherly and protective aspects."

84. *Ibid.*, p. 178.

85. *Hamlet*, IV, iv, 53–56. Cf. *Billy Budd*, XIII, 49–50: "The circumstances that provoke [passion], however trivial or mean, are no measure of its power."

86. *P.L.*, I, 601–604; IX, 171–172.

87. *Moby-Dick*, II, 352, 330.

88. *P.L.*, IV, 393–394.

89. *Moby-Dick*, I, 232, 269–270; cf. I, 310, 314–315 for the prominence of fate in Rodney's doom. Some doubt is cast on the above interpretation of "The Mat-Maker" in Carvel Collins, "Melville's *Moby-Dick*," *The Explicator*, IV (February, 1946), [7].

90. Starbuck's words about the hell within Ahab are very close to Redburn's about Jackson and to White Jacket's about Bland. Starbuck said "In his eyes I read some lurid woe would shrivel me up, had I it" (*Moby-Dick*, I, 211). See the quotations above from *Redburn*, p. 134, and *White Jacket*, p. 233.

91. *P.L.*, IV, 18–23, 73–77.

92. *Moby-Dick*, I, 252.

93. *P.L.*, IX, 463–466.

94. *Moby-Dick*, II, 328–329.

95. *P.L.*, IX, 468.

96. *Moby-Dick*, II, 330.

97. *P.L.*, IX, 467–470, 119–123.

98. *Moby-Dick*, I, 209. Cf. "The Pipe," *Ibid.*, I, 160.

99. *P.L.*, IX, 163–171.

100. *Moby-Dick*, II, 239–240.

101. *Ibid.*, II, 341; I, 190; cf. II, 328. The sorrow of loneliness appears also in *Typee*, p. 310; *Redburn*, p. 359; *Pierre, passim*; *Israel Potter*, p. 123.

102. *P.L.*, II, 426, 509, 632; III, 441–442, 667, 699; IV, 129, 508–511, etc.

103. *Ibid.*, I, 84–87, 605–620.

104. *Moby-Dick*, I, 100, 157; II, 326–330.

105. *P.L.*, I, 56–58, 93–116.

106. *Moby-Dick*, II, 244.

# Chapter Seven
[Pages 105–116]

1. Walter Pater, *Marius the Epicurean* (London, [1934]), p. 131.

2. Most of the known volumes of Melville's library bear inscriptions dated 1860 or later, and these seem to be the dates of acquisition, not of first reading. With one exception, all the association volumes to be mentioned in this section bear dates between 1860 and 1883. The single exception is to my knowledge undatable except for its year of publication, 1824 (Joseph Forsyth, *Remarks on Antiquities . . . in Italy*, Third Edition [London, 1824], 2 vols. Melville's copy, now owned by Mrs. Frances T. Osborne, is on deposit at the N.Y.P.L.

3. *The Poems of Elizabeth Barrett Browning* (N.Y., 1860), 2 vols.; II, 405, 11. 1134–1139 and 1154–1156 of Part One of the poem. Melville's copy, now owned by Mrs. Frances T. Osborne, is on deposit at the N.Y.P.L.

4. Forsyth, *Remarks on Antiquities*, I, 133.

5. Matthew Arnold, *Mixed Essays, Irish Essays, and Others* (N.Y., 1883), pp. 193, 194, 189. Melville's copy is in the Houghton Library.

6. *Ibid.*, p. 194.

7. Isaac Disraeli, *Curiosities of Literature*, ed. B. Disraeli (London, 1859), 3 vols.; II, 225. Melville's copy, now owned by Mrs. Frances T. Osborne, is on deposit at the N.Y.P.L.

8. *Redburn*, pp. 356–357. The quotation includes this passage:

> [*Milton's Satan*] *is not a genuine being, but something altered from a genuine original. We gather not from the four gospels alone any high-raised fancies concerning this Satan. . . . But this takes not from the merit of our high priest of poetry; it only enhances it, that with such unmitigated evil for his material, he should build up his most goodly structure.*

The implications of "high priest" may have been in Melville's mind when he lined Arnold's praise of Milton's "developed spiritual and intellectual order" (Matthew Arnold, *Essays in Criticism* [Boston, 1865], p. 420. Melville's copy is in the Houghton Library). The whole emphasis on the poet's enhancement of the original must have come back to Melville when he read a curious parallel in which Arthur Penrhyn

158

Stanley used Christ instead of Satan. Melville bracketed the verses and underlined six words:

> The battle-field of Israel may have suggested to Him . . . those "victorious deeds" and "heroic acts" which Milton has ascribed to His early meditations:
>
> > "One while
> > To rescue Israel from the Roman yoke,
> > Then to subdue and quell o'er all the earth
> > Brute violence, and proud tyrranic power."
>
> But it is the poet only, not the Evangelist, who has ventured to throw even this passing thought into that peaceful career.

(Arthur Penrhyn Stanley, *Sinai and Palestine* [N.Y., 1863], p. 349. Melville's copy, now owned by Mrs. Frances T. Osborne, is on deposit at the N.Y.P.L. The lines by Milton are from *P.R.*, I, 216–219.)

9. Percy Bysshe Shelley, *Essays, Letters from Abroad, Translations and Fragments*, ed. Mrs. Shelley (London, 1852), 2 vols.; I, 32–33. On pp. 38–39 there is another line by Melville beside a passage which lauds a list of authors that includes Milton. Melville's copy is in the Houghton Library. The applicability to Ahab of the quotation from p. 33 has been noted by Braswell in *Melville's Religious Thought*, p. 69.

10. Arnold, *Essays in Criticism*, pp. 331, 341. The lines by Milton are from *P.L.*, I, 591–594.

11. *Ibid.*, pp. 293, 292. On p. 342 Melville underlined *key* and *verb* in Arnold's discussion of the suspension in *P.L.*, I, 1–6.

12. Homer, *Iliads*, I, xiv, 14. The quotation, which is accurate, is from *P.L.*, I, 711.

13. *Complete Works of Ralph Waldo Emerson*, VIII, 68.

14. *The Poetical Works of Robert Burns*, ed. Gilfillan (Edinburgh, 1856), 2 vols.; II, 70. Melville's copy is in the Houghton Library.

15. *Selections*, ed. Thorp, pp. 338, 424 n. 10.

16. Shelley, *Essays*, I, 33.

17. *White Jacket*, p. 35.

18. *Mardi*, II, 54.

19. "Mr. Parkman's Tour," p. 291.

20. The Review, dated December 3, 1857, is reprinted in Weaver, *Melville*, pp. 371–372.

21. The Review, dated February 3, 1858, is reprinted in "Melville and his Public: 1858," p. 69. The sentence quoted here immediately precedes the one which was quoted above (p. 31) and which contains a quotation from *P.L.*

22. It is difficult to find precisely what authority, if any, Melville had for saying that Roman statuary produced any real effect on Milton. He may have recalled Newton's statement that the poet stayed in Rome, "feasting . . . both his eyes and his mind, and delighted with the fine paintings, and sculptures, and other rarities

and antiquities of the city." Or perhaps his source was Hayley's conjecture that Bandinelli's "two large statues of Adam and Eve . . . might stimulate even by their imperfections the genius of a poet," and of Milton in particular (*Poetical Works of John Milton*, ed. Todd, I, 31–32).

The identification of what Melville thought was a description of the Vatican is as difficult as the problem about statuary. Assuming that he meant the Vatican as a structure, one clue is Todd's suggestion that in the "secret conclave" at the end of the first book of *P.L.* Milton intended a comparison to a meeting of Cardinals after the death of a Pope (*Ibid.*, n. to *P.L.*, I, 795). From that surmise Melville may have moved to the conclusion that Pandemonium itself was based on Milton's memory of the Vatican,

> *a fabrick huge . . .*
> *Built like a temple, where pilasters round*
> *Were set, and Dorick pillars overlaid*
> *With golden architrave; nor did there want*
> *Cornice or freeze* [sic]*, with bossy sculptures graven:*
> *The roof was fretted gold*

[P.L., *I, 710–717; see pp. 30 and 109 for Melville's quotation of l. 711*].

One passage from *P.R.* (IV, 34–38) may also have been the source of both reports—of Milton's interest in statuary and of his description of the Vatican. Satan shows to Christ imperial Rome,

> *With towers and temples proudly elevate*
> *On seven small hills, with palaces adorn'd,*
> *Porches, and theatres, baths, aqueducts,*
> *Statues, and trophies, and triumphal arcs,*
> *Gardens, and groves.*

If the reporter of the statement about the Vatican used words rather loosely, there might be importance in this sentence: "The description of the creation in the third book of *Paradise Lost*, (ver. 708, 719,) is supposed by Mr. Walker to be copied from the same subject as treated by Raphael in the gallery of the Vatican, called 'la Bibbia di Raffaello' " (*Poetical Works of John Milton*, ed. Todd, I, 32).

Whatever was in Melville's mind, he was probably in error if he implied that Milton ever attempted an accurate description of the Vatican, and was almost surely wrong if he believed that he was much influenced by statuary. Milton's interest in the details just quoted from *P.R.*

> *scarcely goes beyond enumeration. To sculpture, for example, there is no other important allusion in the verse, and the two that we find in the prose are primarily introduced for the sake of comparison. . . . This indifference to much of the builder's and the sculptor's work, though here and there partially counteracted in Milton, and though in some measure due to his subject-matter, is of course his by right of birth and calling,*

and by fault of vision, one might add of his later years (Ida Langdon, *Milton's Theory of Poetry and Fine Art* [New Haven, 1924], pp. 36–37).

For a document unknown to Melville, but possibly containing corroboration of

Milton's interest in Greek statuary which he may have observed in Italy, see "Of Statues and Antiquities," *The Works of John Milton*, ed. Frank A. Patterson and others (N.Y., 1931–1938), 18 vols. in 21; XVIII, 258–261.

23.  Geist, *Melville*, p. 64.

24.  Wright, "Biblical Allusion in Melville's Prose," p. 185. On the same page Miss Wright asserts that in the thirteen volumes of Melville's prose in the collected edition, there are approximately 650 references and allusions "to Biblical characters, places, events, and books." This figure cannot be used very satisfactorily for comparison with my figures on Milton because Miss Wright does not distinguish between references and allusions, because our standards for establishing a passage as showing a literary influence would necessarily vary, because her figure may include some passages which are Miltonic rather than Biblical, and because mine cover Melville's verse as well as his prose. ✓

25.  "Hawthorne and His Mosses," XIII, 142.

26.  *Redburn*, p. 357.

27.  *Redburn* appeared probably on September 29, 1849 (Minnigerode, *Personal Letters of Melville*, pp. 140, 143; Michael Sadleir, "Bibliography of the First Editions of the Prose Works of Herman Melville," *Confidence-Man*, pp. 337–358, p. 349). "Hawthorne and His Mosses" appeared on August 17 and 24, 1850 (*The Literary World*, VII, 125–127, 145–147).

28.  *Pierre*, p. 361.

29.  *Confidence-Man*, p. 317. There is, of course, no real contradiction between this statement and the earlier one from *Redburn* (p. 356): "Though Milton's Satan dilutes our abhorrence with admiration, it is only because he is not a genuine being, but something altered from a genuine original." Here the meaning of *original* is close to "appearing for the first time;" in *The Confidence-Man* (p. 318) Melville explains a meaning close to "giving new concepts to the reader":

> The original character, essentially such, is like a revolving Drummond light, raying away from itself all round it—everything is lit by it, everything starts up to it (mark how it is with Hamlet), so that, in certain minds, there follows upon the adequate conception of such a character, an effect, in its way, akin to that which in Genesis attends upon the beginning of things.

30.  These figures are analyzed in greater detail in Appendix C.

31.  *Redburn*, p. 244.

32.  E.g., "Verbal Index to the Poetry of Milton," *Poetical Works of John Milton*, ed. Todd, I, 219 ff.; "[Subject] Index" followed by "Verbal Index," in *Paradise Lost*, ed. Thomas Newton (London, 1750), 2 vols., II, 457 ff.

33.  Review of *Etchings of a Whaling Cruise* and *Sailors' Life and Sailors' Yarns*, p. 106; *Redburn*, p. 220; *White Jacket*, p. 4.

34.  *Moby-Dick*, II, 367; I, 86; II, 283.

35.  *Pierre*, p. 502.

36.  "Piazza," X, 14.

37. *Redburn*, p. 356. Cf. *Billy Budd*, XIII, 49–50.

38. *Moby-Dick*, I, 144, 183; cf. 91–92, 99.

39. "Hawthorne and His Mosses," XIII, 133.

# Appendix A
[Pages 118–119]

1. H.M. to E.A.D., February 24, 1849 (*Selections*, ed. Thorp, p. 370).

2. Two copies of Milton associated with Melville's family are extant. One is an edition published in London in 1843 and owned by Mrs. E. M. Marett, a cousin of Melville's wife. The volume "probably reached the Melville household as late as 1878, after Mrs. Marett's death" (letter to me from Mrs. Eleanor Melville Metcalf, in whose possession the volume is at present). The other is a copy of *Paradise Lost*, London, 1795, which once belonged to Melville's grandfather, Thomas Melvill (*sic*) of Boston. From him it passed through Herman Melville's Aunt Lucy to his sister, Kate M. Hoadley. In 1930 Miss Charlotte Hoadley presented the volume to the Gansevoort-Lansing Collection of the N.Y.P.L.

3. *The Dramatic Works of William Shakespeare* (Boston, 1837), 7 vols. This was a reissue of an 1836 edition.

4. *The Poetical Works of John Milton*, ed. John Mitford (Boston, 1836), 2 vols. This was a reissue of an 1834 edition. The same sizes of type were used in both the Shakespeare and the Milton.

5. *Moby-Dick*, I, 332.

6. See pp. 147, n. 15; 150, n. 65; 159, n. 22; 161, n. 32.

7. *Moby-Dick*, II, 300.

# BIBLIOGRAPHY

*"Is there then all this work to
one book, which shall be read
in a very few hours; and, far
more frequently, utterly skipped
in one second; and which, in the
end, whatever it be, must undoubtedly go to the worms?"*
—Pierre, *p. 424*

THE following list includes only those items which have been referred to in the course of this study. An asterisk is used to indicate a volume from Melville's own library.

Abercrombie, Lascelles: *The Epic*, London, Secker, [1914].

Addison, Joseph: *Criticism on Milton's Paradise Lost, From 'The Spectator,'* ed. Edward Arber, London, English Reprints, 1868.

*Alphabetical and Analytical Catalogue of the New York Society Library*, N.Y., Craighead, 1850.

American Art-Union: *Bulletin* [N.Y.], No. 3, May 25, 1848.

————: *Transactions . . . for the Year 1848*, N.Y., Nesbitt, 1849.

Anderson, Charles Roberts: "The Genesis of *Billy Budd,*" *Am. Lit.,* XII (November, 1940), 329–346.

————: *Melville in the South Seas*, N.Y., Columbia U.P., 1939.

*Arnold, Matthew: *Essays in Criticism*, Boston, Ticknor & Fields, 1865.

*————: *Mixed Essays, Irish Essays, and Others*, N.Y., Macmillan, 1883.

Bezanson, Walter Everett: *Herman Melville's "Clarel,"* unpublished dissertation in Yale University Library, 1943.

Boynton, Percy H.: *Literature and American Life*, Boston, Ginn, 1936.

Bradshaw, John: *A Concordance to the Poetical Works of John Milton*, London, Sonnenschein, 1894.

Braswell, William: "Melville as a Critic of Emerson," *Am. Lit.,* IX (November, 1937), 317–334.

————: *Melville's Religious Thought*, Durham, Duke U.P., 1943.

163

——: "Melville's Use of Seneca," *Am. Lit.*, XII (March, 1940), 98–104.

*Browning, Elizabeth Barrett: *Poems*, N.Y., Francis, 1860, 2 vols.

*Burns, Robert: *Poetical Works*, ed. George Gilfillan, Edinburgh, Nichol, 1856, 2 vols.

Bush, Douglas: *Paradise Lost in Our Time*, Ithaca, Cornell U.P., 1945.

*Catalogue of the A. T. Stewart Collection of Paintings, Sculptures . . .* , Illustrated Edition, N.Y., American Art Association, 1887.

*Channing, William Ellery: *Works*, Eighth Complete Edition, Boston, Munroe, 1848, 6 vols.

*Chapone, Hester Mulso: *Letters on the Improvement of the Mind*, Boston, Wells & Wait, 1809.

*Chatterton, Thomas: *Poetical Works*, Cambridge, Grant, 1842, 2 vols.

Cheever, Rev. Henry T.: *The Whale and His Captors*, N.Y., Harper, 1850.

Collins, Carvel: "Melville's Moby-Dick," *Explicator*, IV (February, 1946), [7].

Colum, Padraic: *A Half-Day's Ride*, N.Y., Macmillan, 1932.

Cook, Reginald L.: "Big Medicine in 'Moby-Dick,' " *Accent*, VIII (Winter, 1948), 102–109.

Craigie, William A.: "The Historical Dictionary of American English," *English Journal*, XV (January, 1926), 13–23.

Davis, Merrell R.: "Melville's Midwestern Lecture Tour, 1859," *Philological Quarterly*, XX (January, 1941), 46–57.

*Dictionary of American Biography*, ed. Allen Johnson and others, N.Y., Scribner, 1928–1937, 20 vols.

*Disraeli, Isaac: *Curiosities of Literature*, ed. B. Disraeli, London, Routledge, 1859, 3 vols.

Editors, The: "Melville and his Public: 1858," *American Notes and Queries*, II (August, 1942), 67–71.

Emerson, Ralph Waldo: *Complete Works*, ed. Edward Waldo Emerson, Centenary Edition, Boston, Houghton Mifflin, 1903–1904, 12 vols.

——: *Journals*, ed. Edward Waldo Emerson and Waldo Emerson Forbes, Boston, Houghton Mifflin, 1909–1914, 10 vols.

**The English Reader*, ed. Lindley Murray, title-page missing, Duyckinck Collection of N.Y.P.L.

——, ed. Lindley Murray, N.Y., Collins, [1802].

Erskine, John: *The Delight of Great Books*, Indianapolis, Bobbs-Merrill, 1928.

Fagin, N. Bryllion: "Herman Melville and the Interior Monologue," *Am. Lit.*, VI (January, 1935), 433–434.

**Fingal*, 2d ed., translated by James Macpherson, London, Becket, 1762.

*Forsyth, Joseph: *Remarks on Antiquities . . . in Italy*, Third Edition, London, Murray, 1824, 2 vols.

Foster, Elizabeth S.: *Herman Melville's "The Confidence-Man,"* unpublished dissertion in Yale University Library, 1942.

Freeman, John : *Herman Melville*, N.Y., Macmillan, 1926.

Geist, Stanley: *Herman Melville: The Tragic Vision and the Heroic Ideal*, Cambridge, Harvard U.P., 1939.

Gleim, William S.: *The Meaning of Moby-Dick*, N.Y., Brick Row Book Shop, 1938.

Hanford, James Holly: "The Dramatic Element in *Paradise Lost,*" *Studies in Philology*, XIV (April, 1917), 178–195.

————: *A Milton Handbook*, Third Edition, N.Y., Crofts, 1941.

Havens, Raymond Dexter: *The Influence of Milton on English Poetry*, Cambridge, Harvard U.P., 1922.

Hawthorne, Julian: *Nathaniel Hawthorne and His Wife*, Boston, Osgood, 1885, 2 vols.

Hawthorne, Nathaniel: *The American Notebooks*, ed. Randall Stewart, New Haven, Yale U.P., 1932.

————: *The English Notebooks*, ed. Randall Stewart, N.Y., Modern Language Association of America, 1941.

Hayford, Harrison: "Two New Letters of Herman Melville," *Journal of English Literary History*, XI (March, 1944), 76–83.

Hillway, Tyrus: "Taji's Quest for Certainty," *Am. Lit.*, XVIII (March, 1946), 27–34.

Homans, George C.: "The Dark Angel: The Tragedy of Herman Melville," *New England Quarterly*, V (October, 1932), 699–730.

*Homer: Iliads*, tr. George Chapman, London, Smith, 1857, 2 vols.

Hunter, Christine Hamilton: *A Study in Herman Melville's Sketches and Tales*, unpublished M.A. essay in Yale University Library, 1941.

Huntress, Keith: "Melville's Use of a Source for *White-Jacket,*" *Am. Lit.*, XVII (March, 1945), 66–74.

Langdon, Ida: *Milton's Theory of Poetry and Fine Art*, New Haven, Yale U.P., 1924.

*Lenox Library Short-Title Lists*, Nos. VIII and XII (1887, 1890).

Lewis, C.S.: *A Preface to Paradise Lost*, London, Oxford U.P., 1942.

*The Literary World*, I–XIII (1847–1853).

*The London Carcanet*, From the Second London Edition, N.Y., Peabody, 1831.

Lowes, John Livingston: *The Road to Xanadu*, Boston, Houghton Mifflin, 1927.

Macready, William C.: "Poetry and Its Influence on Popular Education," *The Literary World*, XI (July 10, 1852), 27–30.

Mansfield, Luther Stearns: *Herman Melville: Author and New Yorker, 1844–1851*, unpublished dissertation in the University of Chicago Library, 1936.

————: "Melville's Comic Articles on Zachary Taylor," *Am. Lit.*, IX (January, 1938), 411–418.

Matthiessen, F. O.: *American Renaissance*, N.Y., Oxford U.P., 1941.

Maugham, Somerset: "Moby Dick," *Atlantic*, CLXXXI (June, 1948), 98–104.

Melville, Herman: *Billy Budd*, ed. F. Barron Freeman, Cambridge, Harvard U.P., [1948].

———: *Herman Melville: Representative Selections*, ed. Willard Thorp, N.Y., American Book, 1938.

———: *Journal of a Visit to London and the Continent, 1849–1850*, ed. Eleanor Melville Metcalf, Cambridge, Harvard U.P., 1948.

———: "Journal of Melville's Voyage in a Clipper Ship," *New England Quarterly*, II (January, 1929), 120–125.

———: *Journal up the Straits*, ed. Raymond M. Weaver, N.Y., Colophon, 1935.

———: *Moby-Dick*, N.Y., Harper, 1851.

———: *Moby-Dick or The White Whale*, Photoplay Title "*The Sea Beast*," N.Y., Grosset & Dunlap, [1925].

———: *Moby-Dick*, ed. Willard Thorp, N.Y., Oxford U.P., 1947.

———: "Mr. Parkman's Tour," *The Literary World*, IV (March 31, 1849), 291–293.

———: "Nathaniel Hawthorne," *Ibid.*, VI (March 30, 1850), 323–325.

———: *Pierre*, ed. Robert S. Forsythe, N.Y., Knopf, 1941.

———: Review of *Etchings of a Whaling Cruise* and *Sailors' Life and Sailors' Yarns*, *The Literary World*, I (March 6, 1847), 105–106.

———: "A Thought on Book-Binding," *The Literary World*, VI (March 16, 1850), 276–277.

———: *The Whale*, London, Bentley, 1851, 3 vols.

———: *Works*, Standard Edition, London, Constable, 1922–1924, 16 vols.

Mencken, H. L.: *The American Language*, Fourth Edition, N.Y., Knopf, 1937.

Milton, John: *Paradise Lost*, ed. Thomas Newton, London, Tonson *et al.*, 1750, 2 vols.

———: *Paradise Lost*, London, Law *et al.*, 1795.

———: *Paradise Lost*, ill. John Martin, London, Tilt, 1833.

———: *Poetical Works*, ed. Henry J. Todd, Second Edition, London, Johnson *et al.*, 1809, 7 vols.

———: *Poetical Works*, ed. John Mitford, Boston, Hilliard, Gray, 1836.

———: *Poetical Works*, ed. David Masson, London, Macmillan, 1882, 3 vols.

———: *Prose Works*, ed. Rufus Wilmot Griswold, Phila., Hooker, 1845, 2 vols.

———: *Works*, ed. Frank A. Patterson and others, N.Y., Columbia U.P., 1931–1938, 18 vols. in 21.

Minnigerode, Meade: *Some Personal Letters of Herman Melville and a Bibliography*, N.Y., Brick Row Book Shop, 1922.

More, Paul Elmer: *Shelburne Essays*, Fourth Series, N.Y., Putnam, 1907.

Mumford, Lewis: *Herman Melville*, N.Y., Literary Guild, 1929.

Murray, Henry A.: "Personality and Creative Imagination," *English Institute Annual, 1942*, N.Y., Columbia U.P., 1943, pp. 139–162.

Myers, Henry Alonzo: *Are Men Equal?*, N.Y., Putnam, 1945.

Odell, George C. D.: *Annals of the New York Stage*, N.Y., Columbia U.P., 1927–1945, 14 vols.

Olson, Charles: *Call Me Ishmael*, N.Y., Reynal and Hitchcock, [1947].

Paltsits, Victor Hugo, ed.: *Family Correspondence of Herman Melville, 1830–1904*, N.Y., N.Y.P.L., 1929.

Parkman, Francis: *The California and Oregon Trail*, N.Y., Putnam, 1849.

Pater, Walter: *Marius the Epicurean*, London, Dent, [1934].

Pommer, Henry F.: "Herman Melville and the Wake of the *Essex*," *Am. Lit.*, XX (November, 1948), 290–304.

———: *Milton's Influence on Herman Melville*, unpublished dissertation in Yale University Library, 1946.

Purcell, James Mark: "Melville's Contribution to English," *Publications of the Modern Language Association*, LVI (September, 1941), 797–808.

Rosenbach, Abraham S. Wolf: *An Introduction to Herman Melville's Moby-Dick*, N.Y., Kennerley, 1924.

Sealts, Merton M.: *Herman Melville's Reading in Ancient Philosophy*, unpublished dissertation in Yale University Library, 1942.

Sedgwick, William Ellery: *Herman Melville: The Tragedy of Mind*, Cambridge, Harvard U.P., 1944.

*Shakespeare, William: *Dramatic Works*, Boston, Hilliard, Gray, 1837, 7 vols.

*Shelley, Percy Bysshe: *Essays, Letters from Abroad, Translations and Fragments*, ed. Mrs. Shelley, London, Moxon, 1852, 2 vols.

*———: *Shelley Memorials*, ed. Lady Shelley, Boston, Ticknor & Fields, 1859.

Simon, Jean: *Herman Melville, Marin, Métaphysicien et Poète*, Paris, Boivin, 1939.

*Stanley, Arthur Penrhyn: *Sinai and Palestine*, N.Y., Widdleton, 1863.

Stewart, Randall: "Recollections of Hawthorne by his Sister Elizabeth," *Am. Lit.*, XVI (January, 1945), 316–331.

Sundermann, K. H.: *Herman Melvilles Gedankengut*, Berlin, Collignon, 1937.

Thorp, Willard: " 'Grace Greenwood' Parodies *Typee*," *Am. Lit.*, IX (January, 1938), 455–457.

Van Doren, Carl: "Lucifer from Nantucket," *Century Magazine*, CX (August, 1925), 494–501.

Watters, R. E.: "Melville's 'Sociality,' " *Am. Lit.*, XVII (March, 1945), 33–49.

Weaver, Raymond M.: *Herman Melville: Mariner and Mystic*, N.Y., Doran, 1921.

Weber, Walter: *Herman Melville, eine stilistische Untersuchung*, Basel, Philographischer Verlag, 1937.

Wegelin, Oscar: "Herman Melville As I Recall Him," *Colophon*, n.s.I (Summer, 1935), 21–24.

Whaler, James: "The Miltonic Simile," *Publications of the Modern Language Association*, XLVI (December, 1931), 1034–1074.

White, Viola: *Symbolism in Herman Melville's Writing*, unpublished dissertation in University of North Carolina Library, 1934.

Wright, Nathalia: "Biblical Allusion in Melville's Prose," *Am. Lit.*, XII (May, 1940), 185–199.

———: *Biblical Allusion in the Prose of Herman Melville*, unpublished M.A. essay in Yale University Library, 1938.

———: *Melville's Use of the Bible*, Durham, Duke U.P., 1949.

*Yankee Doodle*, I–II (1846–1847).

# INDEX

169

H 1